EMBERTON

Joseph Emberton. Royal Corinthian Yacht Club, Burnham-on-Crouch, 1931.
Photograph by Joseph Emberton (?).

EMBERTON

Rosemary Ind

LONDON & BERKELEY
Scolar Press

First published 1983 by
Scolar Press
James Price Publishing Limited
13 Brunswick Centre
London WC1N 1AF
and
2430 Bancroft Way
Berkeley
California 94704

British Library Cataloguing in Publication Data
Ind, Rosemary
    Emberton
    1. Emberton, Joseph   2. Architects—Great
    Britain—Biography
    I. Title
    720'.92'4   NA997.E/

ISBN 0–85967–595–5
ISBN 0–85967–675–7 Pbk

Typeset by Gloucester Typesetting Services.
Printed and bound in Great Britain
at the University Press, Cambridge.

Acknowledgements

My thanks are due to a great many individuals and institutions whose help and kindness made this book possible, above all to Kathleen Emberton and her daughter Jocelyn Underwood for their hospitality and encouragement and for the use of their archive; to Emberton's clients at Blackpool Pleasure Beach, Mr and Mrs Leonard Thompson, and their son the present Managing Director, Geoffrey Thompson; to Simpson Piccadilly Ltd, especially to Peter Southgate and Clare Lincoln; to the Architectural Association and to the Royal Institute of British Architects; to the students of the Open University whose various professions bring to discussion special knowledge; to Emberton's friends and professional associates, especially Serge Chermayeff, R. H. Pearson, Carl-Ludwig Franck, and Godfrey Samuel; to Allan Ure, who was a junior draughtsman in Emberton's office in 1924 and who between 1975 and 1979, when Mr Ure died, explained and demonstrated to me the work of the Burnets, of Tait, of Mackintosh, in one of whose houses he lived, and the early work of Emberton which would otherwise have been forgotten; lastly to the many personal friends whose interest and discussion has been invaluable.

R.I.
February 1983

Introduction

Joseph Emberton's work achieved international recognition in 1932 when his Royal Corinthian Yacht Club at Burnham-on-Crouch was selected for the International Exhibition of Modern Architecture, held at the Museum of Modern Art, New York.

Although Emberton claimed that he never received a single fundamental idea from his teachers, he was a student at the Royal College of Art (then the Kensington College of Art) whilst W. R. Lethaby was Professor of Ornament and Design, and he was to adopt an aesthetic strongly reminiscent of Lethaby's 'Efficiency Style'.

His early office experience with the large London practice of Sir John Burnet, Tait and Lorne brought him into contact not only with the tradition within which Burnet and Tait worked (the Scottish Neo-Classical and the Glasgow Modernist styles) but also with contemporary American and European – notably Dutch – architecture, of which Tait was the earliest exponent in this country. Emberton's earliest commissions in the Twenties, which included pavilions for the British Empire Exhibition at Wembley, Summit House for Austin Reed, and the New Empire Hall, Olympia, reflect this contact, and also assert the influence of Sulleiman architecture which he saw whilst in Egypt with the British Army in 1916.

Emberton's fully developed style maintained the links with advertising and exhibition design which had been fundamental throughout his career. He explored the possibilities of new materials – 'crystal, concrete and chromium' in the Twenties, welded steel, plywood and pre-cast concrete in the Thirties – ornamented by a use of curves and coloured light largely learned from, and equalled only by, the work of Eric Mendelsohn. As well as the Royal Corinthian Yacht Club, Simpson's of Piccadilly and the Casino and Pleasure Beach at Blackpool also must be regarded as mature works of modern architecture. They display an exceptional energy: Simpson's is a sophisticated essay in elegance; Blackpool Casino and the Pleasure Beach, with its architectural sequence of 'scientific toys' a unique Modern Movement fairground.

Emberton's buildings embody the qualities of elegance and exuberance, firmly based in an architecture of reason.

To Kathleen Emberton,
and to Allan Ure of Windyhill, Kilmacolm,
this book is dedicated

Joseph Emberton

Joseph Emberton was born in 1889 in Audley, Staffordshire, a village at the edge of the Cheshire plain, overlooking the industrial landscape of the Potteries. His father kept a draper's shop which supplied the local mining community (1). At the age of seventeen he was articled to Chapman and Snape, local architects to the Five Towns, where he spent his time making surveys, dragging measuring chains, 'the chains of his slavery', around warehouses. In the evenings he rode his bicycle to Burslem Art School, and from there he won the scholarship to the Kensington College of Art in London which was to make possible his long-desired escape from the Midlands.

Twenty-two years old, Emberton arrived in London in 1911 to take up his scholarship (2). The Kensington College of Art was also a school of architecture, but at that time architecture was held low in esteem. Sylvia Pankhurst, a graduate of the painting school, was leading the painting and sculpture students in a protest against the requirement that all students should study architecture, the 'Mother of the Arts'. Perversely, Emberton wrote to the Principal, asking permission to attend extra classes in architectural drawing. This was refused, on the grounds that 'students must learn to keep to arrangements made at the beginning of term'.

Surviving records provide a scanty picture of the structure of the course, although the reputations of the professors give us some clues to the prevalence of late Arts and Crafts, and English Free Style, in the teaching. The Principal was Augustus Spencer, the Professor of Ornament and Design, W. R. Lethaby, and the Professor of Architecture, selected by Lethaby, was Beresford Pite. Pite included among his architectural interests Syrian Early Christian architecture, Dürer, and Michelangelo.[1] His style is demonstrated by a town house at 82 Mortimer Street, London W1 (1896) (3) – a grand, pedimented piano nobile, which supports a small pedimented window, in turn supported by huge Michelangelesque figures. But when Pite was constrained by budget, and by changing taste, as he seems to have been at All Souls' School in Foley Street, London W1 (1906–8) (4), his work is much simpler, and more acceptable to modern taste. The brickwork of the Riding House Street elevation is articulated by four huge, round-headed arches. The fourth arch is singled out for special treatment: it rises half a storey higher than the others and is then interlaced by two secondary arches in low relief – altogether a convincing and refined neo-Byzantine design.

Lethaby was a much more influential figure. Although sympathetic to the aims of William Morris, Lethaby took a positive attitude towards machine art. He proposed to use machinery itself in the struggle to reimpose that excellence of craftsmanship which had been destroyed by the misuse of the machine – a homeopathic remedy for design. As Le Corbusier would later propose the motor-car and the aeroplane as models for an architecture of the machine age,[2] so in 1911 did Lethaby propose the efficiency of a naval squadron – an 'efficiency style'. To this end he suggested that those simple, repetitive processes better performed by machines should be carried out by machines, to act as a foil for sparingly-employed hand-craftsmanship. 'Design', he wrote, 'is as nothing compared with workmanship. The modern way of building must be flexible and vigorous, even smart and hard.'[3] Emberton would seem to have been predisposed to welcome such views, but somehow they failed to reach him. Those two years, he told C. H. Reilly, Roscoe Professor of Art (Architecture) in the University of Liverpool, 'were the dullest of his whole life. From his teachers he never received a single fundamental idea.'[4]

Frederick Etchells, Vorticist painter and, as the architect of offices for Crawford's Advertising Agency in London's High Holborn (1923–29), a Modernist pioneer, was Emberton's near-contemporary at Kensington College of Art, and shared his opinion. 'I was taught by Lethaby, who', he told Richard Cork, 'was good but only interested in the early Italians, and the College was very corrupt, like the Church of England in the 1830s. The Principal was not the slightest bit interested in art.'[5]

In response to a feeling that architects were losing ground in the public esteem, the Board of Architectural Education had been established, and presented its report in 1905. A general principle was laid down that would enable teachers, pupils and the public to tread safely through the 'quicksands of fashion and caprice' in matters of taste. This principle would be based on construction, and a knowledge of construction would protect the professional from the 'mere accidents of style and ornament so precious to the learned amateur'.

In a discussion of the Board's report,[6] C. H. Reilly described some of its findings. A four year course was proposed, the first two of which should be in a school followed by two more as a pupil. The schools were to be equipped with a laboratory or workshop for experiment and the demonstration of actual building processes. More surprisingly, schools were also to have museums of architectural models and materials, but for the purpose of demonstrating that the aptness of defunct ornament had been intrinsic to its own construction system – for analysis rather than as exemplar.

'The student must learn to handle his masses', wrote Reilly, remarking that the students of the Paris Beaux Arts school were far better able to do this than their British contemporaries. At the same time, ornament and detail should be used sparingly. The encouragement of premature originality in detail had led, he wrote, 'to the absurdities of Art Nouveau'. In his opinion, architecture schools should be within the organization of universities, as was his own Department at Liverpool, to ensure the general education of architects, as well as the possibility of changing discipline for those students who proved to lack vocation.

Emberton graduated in 1913 with a Certificate in Architecture. He had aimed for a Diploma, which would have taken him on to the Royal Academy Schools, but his draughtsmanship did not reach the standard – a situation he had foreseen when he had asked for, and been denied, extra classes.

What he had valued at the College was the opportunity to meet students of the applied arts. Percy Metcalf, designer of the Thrift threepenny piece, and of the animals, birds and fishes of the Irish coinage, worked with him over and over again, providing elegant West End design and rumbustious fair-ground ornament with equal success. Emberton also commissioned two other ex-students, Joan Lockey and Margaret Blundell, and the work of these three seemed to be imbued with the influence of Walter Crane – romanticized, simple in outline and consistently two-dimensional: it may also owe something to the Viennese Secession.

Emberton's first job after leaving the Kensington College of Art was with the firm of Trehearne and Norman, who were then designing most of the large office buildings in the newly cut-through Kingsway (opened in 1906). Central House, Imperial House, Regent House, York House; the names reflect their self-confident conformity. Emberton could not have admired their reshuffled ideas; these blocks rely, for what individuality they possess, on giant columns and centrally placed pediments and balconies (5).

But it was at this time that Emberton made the acquaintance of Sir John Burnet (at that time John J. Burnet, to distinguish him from his father, the Glasgow architect, J. J. Burnet) through his junior partner Thomas Tait. Burnet and Tait had just completed Kodak House (1911) (6), also in Kingsway, which had been widely acclaimed, not least by Lethaby and his followers. The client, Eastman Kodak, had refused Burnet's first sketch as not modern enough, and Burnet had responded by visiting America, and returning with a Chicago School veneer to his French Beaux Arts repertoire. A smaller version of the Chicago School office buildings, Kodak House consists of four floors of offices. The elevations are marked by residual soaring columns over a simplified rusticated zone and piano nobile of three central bays flanked by two reduced bays and two full bays set at 45 degrees to the front. The central entrance and ground floor shop windows are framed in black granite, moulded and set with a softly curved keystone. The flat roof's residual cornice, traces of capitals, bases and judiciously set keystones are all that remain of ornamentation.

Although Burnet's own work, and that of his father, must have provided Emberton with sturdy exemplars, he responded more energetically to the more modern taste of Tait. 'It was Tait', wrote Reilly, 'who first made him see that there was something in architecture beyond the pretty pattern of the Orders. It was Tait who made him understand the importance of the relation of one plane to another, and of one mass to another. In short, it was Tait who first gave him some of the fundamental ideas he should have received at South Kensington.'[7]

That Tait was in a position to do this was a product of his own study of the work of Alexander ('Greek') Thomson. Tait's father, a Paisley builder who came from a long line of stone carvers, had apprenticed him to the architect James Donald, at one time Chief Draughtsman in the office of 'Greek' Thomson (1817–75). Donald owned some Thomson drawings which he allowed Tait, himself a fine draughtsman, to copy. Tait went on to be perhaps the first British architect to understand and admire Dutch avant-garde architecture (first showing its influence – notably that of Willem Dudok – in Silver End (7, 8), the garden village being built around 1927 for Crittals, the metal window manufacturers), and there is an unmistakable affinity between the massing of Thomson's magnificent Neo-Classical architecture (9) and the New Architecture of Dudok's Hilversum Town Hall (10).

The pedagogical contribution of Tait and Burnet marks a turning-point in Emberton's career. Burnet's knowledge of the American work of Louis Sullivan (11) and the Chicago School, added to his Parisian Beaux Arts training and con-solidated in his own considerable contribution to architecture, was combined with Thomas Tait's knowledge of Alexander Thomson's capacity for composing with mass, and Willem Dudok's similar (though with De Stijl inflections) compositional technique. Tait's enthusiasm for the Dutch also introduced Emberton to the work of H. P. Berlage (who in turn had introduced the work of Frank Lloyd Wright to Europe). In the late Twenties, the new buildings of Holland were in advance of those of most of the rest of Europe, and Tait was responsible for Emberton's exposure to them. Thus Tait provided Emberton not only with the tradition he needed, but also with new models designed by his contemporaries.

At the outbreak of war in 1914 Emberton left Trehearne and Norman to enlist in the territorial regiment of the City of London, The Honourable Artillery Company. He was posted first to Catterick Camp, and from there to Egypt, where he served in 1916 as a gunner.

Emberton's tour of duty in Egypt, like Le Corbusier's travels in the Middle East, provided him with first-hand examples of a new architecture – a plastic architecture readily applicable to the new plastic material, reinforced concrete. The forms of Egyptian plastered mud buildings – especially those of the Ottoman Emperors, the Sulleimans – demonstrated in a manner which could not have been foreseen Tait's teachings on mass and the conjunction of masses. Emberton's first independent work, at the British Empire Exhibition of 1924–25, was to embody both Tait's teaching and the 'lesson of Egypt'.

Immediately after the war, his regiment prepared for its new posting to India, whilst Emberton, wounded and in hospital, took stock of his position. He would have liked to rejoin his regiment in India, but for this he would need private means. Reluctantly he decided to return to architecture, and accepted a place in Sir John Burnet's office where Tait, recently returned from war service at Woolwich, was also working.

When, therefore, Emberton finally made up his mind to be an architect, 'it was as an architect with a mission. He would give the architecture of our own day a new logic. It should be in his hands the means of interpreting the laws of nature rather than the manners of mankind. Of the reliability of the latter the war had provided him with sufficient evidence.'[8]

Arriving in Burnet's offices late in 1918, Emberton joined Tait who, with Burnet, was working on the design for Adelaide House (1920–25) (12), the large office building on the north side of London Bridge. Like Kodak House, its precursor, Adelaide House expresses in its facade the rhythm of the underlying steel skeleton, though here there is a visual ambiguity, the vertical members, the 'columns', being twice as numerous as the underlying steel stanchions. At river level, one storey below the road, the rhythm is determined by four huge, Sullivanesque, trabeated arches. Above this 'rusticated zone' the building is resolved into two main elevations and the rhythm of the five bays is subdivided to form a pattern of window bays. Each elevation, one to the street, the other to the river, is expressed separately and then 'tied in' to the central volume by means of darker bands of masonry. Horizontals and verticals are balanced in what is just *not* a Beaux Arts symmetry, betraying the building's allegiance to Modernism.

As with many buildings, the decorative details are more modish than the form: the entrance railings are reminiscent of the work of C. R. Mackintosh (Tait had been a student at Mackintosh's Glasgow School of Art) or even that of Frank Lloyd Wright; and the panels of incised ornament have an Egyptian flavour.

Emberton approved of the simplified design, and Allan Ure, who was a draughtsman both in Burnet's office and later in Westwood and Emberton's, suggests that Emberton had a hand in its production.[9] The block-like volume and the Egyptian-ate ornament certainly reappear in his work with Percy Westwood at Wembley.

In 1922 Emberton left the practice of Burnet, Tait and Lorne and went into partnership with Percy Westwood, in whose office he had worked temporarily early in 1918. Westwood, who had a practice that specialized in shop design, had just completed two exhibition stands for Imperial Chemical Industries, and he passed to Emberton a commission for two more. Donald Hope, the advertising manager for ICI, introduced Emberton to Sir Lawrence Weaver.

Weaver was the editor of *Country Life*, which styled itself '*The* journal for all interested in Domestic Architecture'. In this capacity he also edited the Country Life Library, which published Gertrude Jekyll, with whom he also collaborated. His own 'Small Country Houses of Today' (c. 1912) illustrated the work of Philip Webb, Baillie Scott, Gimson and Barnsley, Lutyens, Voysey and Edgar Wood.

Weaver, in 1922, had just been appointed Director of British Exhibits for the British Empire Exhibition at Wembley (1924–25) and in this role he commissioned two stands from Westwood and Emberton, which Emberton designed. Weaver was delighted; 'stand after stand followed, each less architectural in the old decorative sense and more architectural in the new expressive way than the last'.

On the subject of exhibitions, Weaver was passionate; as editor of *Country Life*, he attended both the 1922 exhibition in Munich, and the Gothenburg exhibition of 1923, 'with sustained pleasure', he said, 'and without fatigue, because my eye and mind were soothed by the seemliness of the setting. I believe that the outrageous weariness that has been regarded as inevitable in ordinary exhibitions in England is partly the result of the air of garish muddle that invests them.'[10]

Of the new work at Wembley, Weaver found 'Mr Emberton's musical instrument section, austere and satisfactory', and his Nobel Industries Hall 'in some ways the most successful thing in the place, for here Emberton has been content simply to emphasise the big lines he found' – sophisticated restraint for a first commission. Few visual records of the exhibition remain, which makes the immediacy of Weaver's comments especially valuable. But the Lakeside and Main Avenue kiosks (13–21) – the last echoes of Secessionism together with the result of Emberton's time in Egypt – *were* recorded, and collected by Weaver in his book *Exhibitions and the Art of Display*.[11] Small, white and severely sculptural and with, for this exhibition, an appropriately Imperial flavour, the Lakeside kiosks form an avenue of pleasure pavilions. The designs are varied; most are slightly battered in outline and have a joggled parapet, with a flat roof, a dome or a barrel vault, and either an inset or a jutting balcony. There are simplified columns which mark entrances – always central. Some kiosks are painted, not always with marked success: the *Daily Telegraph*'s gothic script sits uncomfortably on that kiosk's cubic simplicity (13).

After Wembley there are rumours of a pavilion at the Exposition International des Arts Décoratifs, held in Paris in 1925. The official catalogue does not list Westwood and Emberton, although other Wembley architects, notably Sir E. Owen Williams and Burnet, Tait and Lorne appear (as do the 'Pavilions of Revolt' – Melnikov's Soviet Pavilion and Le Corbusier's *Pavilion de l'Esprit Nouveau*). Kathleen Emberton recalls her husband's kiosk, 'very small, and very prettily lit'.[12]

The language set up at Wembley, particularly that expressed in the Kensitas kiosk (14, 15), reappears in 1926 in a house built in Weybridge for Mrs Ian Anderson (22–25). Anderson, a City of London stockbroker, also commissioned interiors for his office in the City, and his Baker Street flat, and furniture for all three. In the Weybridge house the mushroom curve of the Kensitas kiosk reappears in the sun-room door.

The plan is for a five-bedroomed house, designed as a long rectangle with a drawn-forward porch, and a parabolic-curved central hall. From this hall opens the drawing room (also drawn slightly forward), dining room, sitting room pantry, scullery and stores. A large lounge balances the drawing and dining rooms and extends into the sun room with the 'Kensitas' door.

In elevation the pitched roof dips down to the one-storey porch in front and the sun room at the side, in the softly curved manner of thatch. This is made possible by the use of cedar shingles steamed into shape on the site to the distinctive curves of the roof. The walls are finished in pebble-dash, reminiscent of harled stone – favourite material of Northern Arts and Crafts architects – and a chimney is given prominence on the front elevation, also in an Arts and Crafts manner.

The construction is a mixture of load-bearing brick walls externally, and reinforced-concrete walls to the curved hall and bedrooms above, with what seem to be reinforced-concrete floors. This is a very eccentric combination. Was the architect using concrete to allow the use of curves or to give a freedom to planning impossible if all the loads were to be transmitted through brick? Is it a retreat from 'logic', or its application in a way that seemed logical at the time? Was it the result of a different approach by Westwood? The stylistic overtones of the building range from the Arts and Crafts of England and Scotland to the Secessionist architecture of Vienna and Darmstadt. J.-M. Olbrich's Villa Friedmann near Vienna (1898) (26) uses a remarkably similar door. The battering of the outline of the Weybridge porch is the precursor of the line of entrance doors at Olympia (1929) and at the same time quotes the Egyptianate pavilions at Wembley. Emberton is assembling the vocabulary of forms which will ultimately become his architectural handwriting, but the house, although eccentric, is harmonious and charming.

Son of a shopkeeper, Emberton was introduced to shop design by his partner Percy Westwood. Westwood (1878–1958) came of a tailoring family. Austin Reed was a personal friend, and Reed's first shop was Westwood's first job. Westwood lived in Weybridge and travelled daily to London with Austin Reed who, by 1925, had prospered to the extent of a headquarters office building, Summit House (1925), in Red Lion Square, Holborn, and a large West End shop (1926) in the newly rebuilt Quadrant of Regent Street, both designed by Westwood and Emberton.

Austin Reed's shop in Regent Street is a hybrid. The Crown retains control of the design of the facades of the street, and Westwood and Emberton were compelled by a trick of fate to work within the design for the elevation provided by one of the most outspoken critics of Modernism, Sir Reginald Blomfield, and to pay him a fee for it.

Behind Blomfield's facade the partnership was breaking down. Westwood told his sons: 'Joe worked by night, I worked by day, no basis for partnership', and Austin Reed's seems to reflect this. Superficially the store was organized in a series of rooms, each of a different style – 'Chinese', 'Tudor', 'Modern'. Only the lift gates seem to be unselfconsciously of their time; Percy Metcalf's metal-work is fair and square in the Ruhlmann style of Paris 1925.

But underneath all this the design for the shop seems to be based on American practice – what Emberton called 'scientific salesmanship'. In an article, 'Modern

Store Design',[13] Emberton illustrated the plans of Austin Reed's parallel with American examples. The ground floor of Daniel Burnham's Wanamaker Building, Philadelphia, demonstrates, he says, much larger 'cells' than were permitted under the fire regulations of the London Building Act. Ely Jacques Kahn's Bonwit Teller Store, New York, shows a 'good arrangement of glass counters and low unit fixtures'. Austin Reed's has the same arrangement: glass counters hug the walls, and small oval display tables interrupt the passage of customers, inviting them to inspect and handle the merchandise. Emberton referred frequently to the restrictions imposed by the London Building Act. He admired the glass canopy of the Galleries Lafayette in Paris, illuminated from within its thickness, and the lofty central space of the store, impossible in London at that time, which 'produces a fine architectural impression on a grand scale at the entrance to a building' and suggests an invitation to the public to inspect the displays without the obligation to buy. At Austin Reed's, Westwood and Emberton conveyed something of this idea with a central well which allows glimpses of the floor above, and they sought to draw customers through the store by the judicious positioning of departments.

In the same article, Emberton praised Selfridges (1909, F. Atkinson, with what Pevsner calls the 'big booming voice' of the American Daniel Burnham as consultant).[14] The original unit, he wrote, was designed with such a sense of scale that it was possible to repeat it over and over again, allowing the building to grow. Its 'one big simple idea' represented a consistency of purpose not to be found in other London stores.

At Summit House, Austin Reed's office building (27), Westwood and Emberton turned by contrast to a European model – Berlage's Holland House, Bury Street in the City of London (1914–16) (28–30). The London office of a Dutch shipping firm designed by the architect of Amsterdam's Stock Exchange, Holland House in this setting is exotic, and its influence in England, apart from that exerted upon Westwood and Emberton, is minimal. The corner which announces the building's presence as it is approached through narrow mediaeval lanes is massed and orchestrated in a manner at once novel and audacious. In the style of the Amsterdam Stock Exchange, the corner is carved and moulded here into an Expressionist ship's prow in black marble. As if to recover from this extravagance, the street elevations are elegantly restrained, again in the manner of the flat wall planes of the Stock Exchange.

The windows are so closely set that the structural verticals dividing them become structural window mullions. These and the coffered panels under the windows are clad in blue-green faience tiles, but the vertical mullions are moulded to stand out from the window plane. Seen in perspective, the only possible view in the narrow street, these seem to collapse visually into a flat wall plane which shimmers like blue-green watered silk.

At Summit House, Westwood and Emberton were faced with the same problem as at Adelaide House, the junction of two facades in a building that has, for practical purposes, only two sides. They attempted to strengthen (or celebrate) the junction by the insertion of a stair tower at the corner and by the asymmetrical massing of the top of the tower with the stepped heights of the two abutting facades. The device is not entirely satisfactory – the stair is compositionally too small and the bay window too narrow – but the attempt is worthy of applause. What is entirely successful is the quotation, in the side elevation, of a simplified version of Berlage's magnificent blue faience wall.

In 1926, the year of the General Strike, Emberton opened his own office in Regent Street. He married Kathleen Marie Chantry, with whom in the previous year he had visited the Exposition International des Arts Décoratifs in Paris.

For some time this visit had repercussions in Emberton's work: the Ruhlmann-like metal-work of the lift gates at Austin Reed's in Regent Street (31) was repeated in the wrought-iron and glass facade of a small and elegant hat shop for Madelon Chaumet (1928, Berkeley Street) (32). The coloured glass friezes of a chain of shoe shops for Lotus and Delta bore witness to the fact that 'we all fell in love with Lalique'.[15] It also gave rise to an exchange between Emberton and F. R. Yerbury, the Secretary of the Architectural Association, at a debate in May 1929. 'Why', challenged Yerbury, 'by buying a crate of glass in Paris and hanging it round a shop front in Edinburgh are you "modern"?' Emberton, recognizing his Lotus and Delta shops in the challenge, replied: 'I would like to ask Mr Yerbury when he heard me say that I was a Modernist?' but continued, 'If we set out to do a job well we shall take things further than they have been taken for some time.'[16]

In 1927 a committee which included Sir Lawrence Weaver appointed Emberton architectural director of the Advertising Association's first exhibition. The layout, four streets of Egyptianate kiosks with low garden walls, was admired by the architectural press for its orderliness (33–36). As at Wembley, the white walls are used as a background for advertising, while the 'garden walls', decorated with cut-out shapes and inscribed lines, seem to bear more relation to the early reinforced concrete design of Perret or Tony Garnier, or to that of Lurçat or

Mallet Stevens, than to the heroic modern architecture then being built at the Weissenhof exhibition in Stuttgart.

But a new decorative element is introduced, a system of parallel 'shelves', used again at Blackpool in 1935, which can act as a horizontal compositional element, a light-baffle, or as air inlet in an air-conditioning system (**34, 35**). The device seems to originate in Eric Mendelsohn's work – his 'trenches sketches', his Berliner Tagblat Building addition (1921–22) and his Schocken store at Stuttgart (1926–27) – and in 1929 Emberton was recommending to readers of the London *Evening News*[17] the buildings of Mendelsohn, of Russia and of Germany. 'London's Buildings Should Tell the Truth' ran the headline, illustrated by Mendelsohn's Einstein Tower and three of his trenches sketches (**37**), fantastic drawings of buildings made during the war, and exhibited in 1919 as 'Architecture in Steel and Concrete'.[18]

The chain of shops for Lotus and Delta shoes (**38**), all with applied design by Percy Metcalf, continued to explore the style of the Paris Exhibition of 1925, but a tools shop for Allen–Liversidge (1929), like Olympia of the same year, stands at the cross-roads of Emberton's maturity. After his flirtation with Paris '25 styling, his work changed direction. A shop selling welding equipment and oxyacetylene cutting tools is obviously no place for frivolous Parisian *chic*, and instead the 'Fitness for Purpose' demands of the shop are met (**39**).

Frederick Towndrow, in a lengthy and enthusiastic review of the building written at the time,[19] compared it with the shop design of Paris and Germany. Shop-fronts, he wrote, were once part of the general architectural whole. The modern shop-front reacts faster and faster to the fashion of the moment, and the 'smart' and 'catchy' is tacked onto the front by an army of shop fitters; the architect scarcely comes into the field. This, he wrote, is especially true of London, 'where a debased version of "Modernist" has come into vogue without any consideration for reticence, scale or proportion'.

'Reticence, scale and proportion' was exactly what Emberton supplied. If his earlier shop-front work had been, as Towndrow said, a 'little affected by the French decorative manner', this one was to be carried out in 'an engineering manner'. The Allen–Liversidge front was constructed in 'Staybrite' stainless steel, with a blue linoleum floor, and red lettering on a horizontal, three-dimensional illuminated 'cornice'. The cornice continued inside the shop as an obscured glass screen which passed around the whole showroom, with engravings of welding and electric lighting processes – once again by Percy Metcalf.

19

By this time Emberton's reputation was growing. William Crabtree, one of the designers of Peter Jones's Chelsea store (1936), arrived in London from C. H. Reilly's department in Liverpool to work for Emberton, 'then big in the modern field'.

The first drawings for a large new project, the New Empire Hall for the exhibition site at Olympia in West London, must have been in preparation then. Crabtree and P. J. Freeman, those 'two fine Liverpool draughtsmen' as Reilly called them,[20] were responsible for the perspective drawings. These show a large white block with deeply incised horizontal window strips flanking a central, even more deeply incised, vertical bay. An aquatint by H. T. Brock Grigg (40) shows the same scene at an earlier stage.[21]

In the constructed version, the 'old-fashioned' appearance of the extreme centrality is modified by some highly eclectic elements. The white front retains a granite-faced rusticated zone and a slightly battered band of entrance doors. The top right-hand corner of the building is 'carved' like a Berlage corner, or like Tait's work at Silver End, and the left-hand corner, seen from the West, even without the effect of a fortuitously placed lamp standard, seems to quote the corner windows of Mendelsohn's Einstein Tower (1919) (41–43). The plan is simple, a grid of fifty-foot squares arranged asymmetrically around the central stairs and lifts, and marked on the elevation by the horizontal element. The windows on the outer face of the wall are a series of lenses, those on the inner face a series of prisms. This arrangement is said to take the light from an angle of 45 degrees from the vertical and to transmit it slightly below the horizontal into the building.

The monumental front to Hammersmith Road is constructed in steel, brick-faced, rendered and painted white. The brick manufacturer's advertisement reads: 'Even when a building is of the ultra modern style associated with concrete construction, brick is standard today'.[22] Emberton must have winced at 'ultra modern', and at the naive acceptance of double standards. 'Ultra modern', he wrote, 'is a horrid label and indicates eccentricity which is detrimental to anything. Modern architecture, being based on reason rather than sentiment, will appeal to the reason of future generations.'[23]

Olympia was much disliked by Henry-Russell Hitchcock who referred, in his accompanying commentary to the 'Modern Architecture in England' exhibition,[24] to the misuse of the example of so sound a building as Jan Wils's Olympic stadium in Amsterdam (1928) (44). But whereas there are resemblances between the stadium and Olympia, and between elements of Olympia and elements of the work of other architects, as has been discussed, Olympia is also a natural consequence of Summit House. However, Hitchcock's comment is timely, since it is probable that Emberton had visited Holland recently. 'He knows Holland' ran an account of Universal House (1933) in the Dutch periodical, *Den Acht en Opbouw*, 'and has visited the Van Nelle Factory [1929] and the Open Air School in Amsterdam [1929–30]'.[25]

But popularly Olympia was a success and, in general, widely praised. 'Please send me the photos and designs of your splendid Olympia house', wrote the editor of *Der Baumeister*; and 'We feel sure you will allow us to make use of your ideas as incorporated in the blueprints,' optimistically persuaded the President of the Zagreb Sample Fair. Emberton must have approached his new commission, for the Royal Corinthian Yacht Club's new clubhouse, in a mood of self-confidence.

It is a nice irony that two buildings with strong Classical overtones to their names, Olympia and Royal Corinthian, were to establish Emberton as a Modernist, try as he would to escape the label.

The Royal Corinthian Yacht Club, named after the ancient Greek games held at the Isthmus of Corinth in honour of the god Poseidon, was founded in 1872 as an amateur sailing club.

The first clubhouse, as befits a London club, was situated on the lower reaches of the Thames at Erith, but the Club soon moved to Port Victoria on the Isle of Grain. The clubhouse at Port Victoria, an Edwardian 'Tudor' villa, did not meet with the approval of the members since, in spite of its beautiful name, the Isle of Grain was an industrial slum, the anchorage was bad, the tides dangerous, the mud foul and the mosquitoes vicious.

In 1914 the Port Victoria house was commandeered by the Admiralty, to nobody's regret, and at the end of the war the Club began to operate again with a small branch house on the Essex estuary of the River Crouch. In 1929, land was obtained on the river wall at Burnham on which to expand the existing clubhouse. This was a small, rectangular, horizontal-boarded timber building in the Essex vernacular style, with a short balcony on the riverside.

At a 'palace revolution' (according to Cyril Goodman[26]) a new Commodore, a new Vice Commodore and eight new members were elected, and the pressing issue to be decided was whether to extend the old clubhouse or start afresh. Less pressing was the question of admitting lady members in their own right.

The new Commodore, Philip Benson of Benson's Advertising, must have been acquainted with Emberton through the Advertising Exhibition of 1927, and when, by a small majority, it was decided to build a new clubhouse, Benson approached Emberton.

The first designs were being prepared in November 1929, and a perspective drawing by William Crabtree for 'An Essex Yacht Club by Joseph Emberton' (45) was shown at the Royal Academy Summer Exhibition of 1930 (No. 1302). This shows a two-storey building, apparently five bays wide. The three central bays step forward to a waterside terrace, from which two flights of steps go down to the water. The columns and floors appear to be of reinforced concrete, and the walls, the parapet, and the parapet of the first-floor balcony, seem to be of brick or weatherboarding – only horizontal bands are drawn. Large windows would have given members the opportunity to enjoy the magnificent river views.

To anyone familiar with British building in the late Twenties, the other exhibits in the R. A. Summer Exhibition reflect the design doldrums of that time: Sir Giles Gilbert Scott's Liverpool Cathedral, Sir Herbert Baker's India House in the Aldwych, London, and Sir Reginald Blomfield's 'The Headrow' in Leeds, are not more than pot-boilers. Of the anti-Establishment, Adams, Holden & Pearson's Southend General Hospital, J. M. Easton & Howard Robertson's Daniel Neal, Kensington High Street, and Oliver Hill's houses in North Street, Westminster are no less second rate. The first perspective, exhibited at the Royal Academy, might have passed unnoticed in this company; the final version would not. It speaks clearly of Lethaby's 'efficiency of a naval squadron – an efficiency style.'

Emberton had just returned from a holiday in Biarritz, where he had been celebrating the completion of Olympia. Whether newly charged with energy from the holiday he took over the project from his assistants, or whether he had been influenced by new building in France or Spain, the new design was a complete surprise to England. Although the new version – eventually the constructed version – retained, with the addition of a third floor, much the same accommodation as before, it seemed to embody a new, or a more definite, brief. The archives of the Club record that Philip Benson approached Emberton for 'a large three-storeyed ferro-concrete structure of advanced design'. So it may have been Benson's advanced ideas, or even those of the members who, as sailors, may have stopped at the new Spanish sailing club at San Sebastian (Labayen and Aizpurua, 1929), which were responsible for one of the first expressions in England of the 'New Spirit'.

The Yacht Club, a reticent, white-skinned, three-storey building with narrow, horizontal clerestory windows, sits on a concrete platform supported on stilts in the water, and on the river wall behind (46, 47). On the riverside the windows step down to floor level and the building stands forward in a double-storeyed glass box, and then extends one step further into wide balconies with two straight flights of steps down to the water. The waterfront, all glittering glass, reflects passing cloud forms and provides grandstand views up and down the wide, flat expanse of the estuary. The back, North, elevation has only the minimum of openings. An early drawing (48)[27] shows a three-storey building of six uneven bays, with bands of continuous windows on two floors, but a row of punched-out windows on the top floor. A tall, thin stair tower with a central vertical window on one side and a grand, stepped entrance towards the other wide, completes the composition.

The constructed version is more elegant. The small, squarish windows on the top floor have been swept into a single glass band that terminates against the carefully placed verticals of the windows of what has become the second stair-case (49, 50). All through the building the constructional fact of the steel frame and lightweight external wall is made visible. As at Olympia, when a window turns a corner, the set-back plane of the steel is apparent, nowhere more so than in the service stair which runs along the inside of the East wall. The steel beam which supports the stair also forms the window opening – therefore the window is on the same diagonal as the stair. On the elevation, four diagonal windows sweep down the wall, turn into the horizontal, round the corner, and drop to make visual contact with the horizontals of the North wall.

The accommodation consists of a 'mixed lounge', a 'mixed dining room', an (unmixed) billiards room, secretary's room and lounge bar on the ground floor; men's lounge, men's dining room, steward's room, card room and library on the second floor, and ten bedrooms and a dormitory on the top floor (51–54). On the roof, a starter's box is reached from the main balconies by way of a cast-iron spiral stair (55), and a set of racing numbers shamelessly ornaments the flat roofline.

'Royal Corinthian' was published in *Country Life* by Emberton's old friend and client Sir Lawrence Weaver, where it was seen by a writer in the Dutch *Bou-kundig Weekblad Architectura*.[28] A white, rendered building without a roof, ran the report, is as striking in an English periodical, as a brick house *with* a roof in a comparable German magazine.

In 1932 the first Exhibition of Modern Architecture, the exhibition of the architecture of the so-called International Style, was held at the Museum of

Modern Art, New York. The American organizers of the exhibition, Henry-Russell Hitchcock and Philip Johnson, collected the work of the Weissenhof architects and that of their Modernist contemporaries and disciples, and gave the whole the somewhat over-simple title of 'The International Style'. The sub-title, 'architecture since 1922', gave more useful information, and allowed the inclusion of some American moderns – Richard Neutra, on account of his Viennese roots, and eventually Frank Lloyd Wright himself.

Amongst this international company, 'Royal Corinthian' appeared with a ludicrously earnest caption: 'The large glass area is particularly suitable in a dull foggy climate.' (Burnham-on-Crouch holds a high place in the league of sunshine record holders.)

In November 1929 the architect Philip Johnson cabled to Emberton for photographs of the Burnham Yacht Club. With the photographs Emberton sent a description, and his correspondence with Johnson makes clear his intentions. 'It is a steel-framed structure, carried on reinforced-concrete piles. The walls are $4\frac{1}{2}$ in. hollow bricks, rendered externally and internally plastered. Although the building is in one of the most exposed positions in this country, up to now it has been quite weatherproof. There are magnificent views on three sides of the Clubhouse . . . and this accounts for the fact that practically three sides of all the main rooms are wholly of glass. The views from the back of the building are poor, merely over a considerable expanse of marshland, and in order to reduce heat losses, windows on the landside have been reduced to a minimum . . . with regard to cost – the building worked out much cheaper than a building of more archaic form of construction.' Johnson replied: 'There are of course some things . . . which do not please me completely, such as the extraordinarily bad circular staircase which you were probably forced to use because it is standardised.' Emberton agreed: 'I am afraid the staircase was imposed upon me on account of the necessity for economy . . . none of the standardised articles which one sees in builders' merchants' catalogues have yet shed their Victorian details and these are in evidence in the detail of the staircase.' The Victorian detail, a hand-some scroll moulding which bothers them both, may be evidence of the influence of John Ruskin. Ruskin argued that wrought iron, cut and twisted by the work-man, is beautiful in proportion to the handiwork embodied in it. Of cast iron, the opposite is true.[29] Johnson continued: 'I also feel that the slanted row of windows in the stair wall does not compose well arranged as you have them'. Here Emberton made a stand: 'I cannot agree with you with regard to the staircase windows for here again the same construction has determined their form. The building', he reiterated, 'has a steel framed structure, the walls are only $4\frac{1}{2}$ in. thick hollow bricks and therefore incompetent to carry loads. With the arrangement of the windows as carried out it was possible for the steel stringer which carried the stair also to carry the panel walls. Again it would be very undesirable to pierce such thin panel walls with window openings not framed up with steel' (56).

Emberton's attention at this time was very much occupied with the 'logic and reason' of wall construction: the glass wall of Universal House, Southwark Bridge (1933), is the result of careful consideration of the functional requirements of walls in what was then the soot-charged air of London. Built in the year after the Daily Express building in Fleet Street (1932, Ellis and Clark, Structural Engineer Sir E. Owen Williams), its construction system benefited from the experience of that building.

Universal House, office and drawing-office building for the exhibition contractors Beck and Pollitzer (57, 58), represents Emberton's most daring experiment with a new material – not so much the glass, as the material for fixing it, 'Birmabright' anodized aluminium alloy. That the experiment was not entirely successful is perhaps borne out by the fact that subsequently, with one exception, he abandoned the glass wall.

Certainly there was some material failure, as there had been in the similar glass wall of the Daily Express Building. Universal House was a flat-roofed, three-storeyed concrete, crystal and chromium building (Emberton's favourite combination at this time) situated on the South side of Southwark Bridge. On the Thames side it dropped, like Adelaide House, two storeys to wharf level so that the main entrance was from the bridge and the service entrance from below. Three storeys of strip windows with green glass horizontal bands running between them swept round, curved out to form the entrance which was also marked by the building's name in handsome blue neon letters, and curved again, round a corner to the riverside. Here the strips were 'caught', and terminated in an opaque stair tower in which the windows were positioned to run counter to the main window strips.

The glass was secured, in a mastic bedding, by strips of aluminium alloy fixed to teak grounds. A pale-green opalescence resulted from the rough rolled glass backed with asbestos sheet which formed the horizontal band between the windows. A detail drawing of this bears a telling note: 'Mastic and portion of ground removed for ventilation to back of glass.' The opalescent glitter was spoilt at close quarters by beads of condensation forming between the glass and its backing, and the provision of ventilation would, it was hoped, prevent this. It was intended to extend the building both upwards and Westwards to connect with a warehouse building that still remains. A watercolour by Robert Millar (**59**) shows this extension, three added storeys on the same lines, and three top ones gradually set back and furnished with balcony rails. Universal House belongs to a group of glass-walled buildings which were being built in England and Scotland at this time. Peter Jones's, Sloane Square (1936, Crabtree, Stater and Moberley in association with C. H. Reilly), Daily Express, Fleet Street (1930–32), Daily Express, Manchester (1938, also by Ellis and Clark with Owen Williams), another Daily Express building, in Glasgow, this time by Owen Williams alone (1936), and Owen Williams's celebrated Boots' Factory at Beeston, Nottingham (1930–32).

They all probably resulted from the desire to provide the maximum of natural light, together with a self-cleaning wall, which coincided with the newly available, more or less dependable flexible strip. Raymond McGrath, in his *Glass in Architecture and Decoration*,[30] uses a typical Modernist argument, that the new use of glass is as suitable for plate glass as was eighteenth-century use, with glazing bars, for Crown glass. Certainly at this time there was a great enthusiasm for glass, which may have come through Mendelsohn's connection with Expressionism (**60**) and the Expressionist architects' delight in sparkle and crystalline form – Bruno Taut's Alps, crowned with cut-glass excrescences and transformed into Berlin, London and Manchester street architecture.

During the 1930s Emberton's commissions continued to consist mainly of shops and exhibitions, with one exception, a Mendelsohn-like project for a speedway track at Skegness, Lincolnshire. A Marble Arch shop for the furriers Style and Mantle (1930) imposed on the customer an architectural promenade through curved-glass display windows.

The Ardath Reminder Shop, Regent Street (1931) (**61, 62**), for gifts exchanged for cigarette coupons, extended the same device. The customer, gift coupon in hand, is enclosed by baroque glass finials which draw him from the street, and the glittering prizes of consumerism lead him up the showcase-lined stair and deliver him at the counters. Once above, positive space (the passage) becomes negative space (the counters). Here are the lighting baffles only hinted at in the 1927 Advertising Exhibition. 'There is intensity of light, without any glare, there is a sparkle with evenness of illumination. Colours and materials are all simple and not unduly costly, but the general effect is one of richness; terrazzo, sycamore, plywood, stainless steel, cellulose, enamels, and glass are set off by groups of descriptive lettering. As a piece of design it has a unity in curvilinear grace and delicacy that appeals equally to the eye and to the intelligence.'[31]

'Curvilinear grace' characterized too the Advertising Exhibition of 1933. Emberton, once again in charge, made great advances on the selfconsciously 'modern' of the exhibition of 1927. The exhibition of 1933 was held, like that of 1927, at Olympia, but whereas in 1927 Emberton had laid out the hall like an American city, on a gridiron plan, by 1933 his 'townscape', though still regular, utilized diagonal 'streets' impinging on central 'fountains' and culminated, as in 1927, with a Praetorium or Town Hall at the head of the Main Avenue **(63)**. The diagonal grid allowed an intricate collection of forms of different size which accumulated to form a harmonious whole. The style consists of the simplest round columns without base or capital, on which sits a flat, table-like roof, with curved corners. In plan the roofs resembled rounded shortbread biscuits fitted loosely into a box. He still uses the flanged 'streamlining' introduced in 1927, but now it is far more controlled. Curved planes detach themselves from the main wall, and are supplied with separate support, sometimes a simple column, sometimes an oval 'elephant's leg', sometimes a curved wall. The British Poster Advertising Association's stand **(64)** had a curved-in-plan external stair which also had a curved-in-elevation solid balustrade topped by a free-running metal handrail. The 'Town Hall' building **(65)** was ornamented by stylized painted figures, but otherwise the names on the stands, the owners' posters and a continuous band of posters running round three sides of the hall provided the only decoration.

But, like Mendelsohn, Emberton knew when to restrain his enthusiasm for curved form. His BTH Refrigerator shop (1931) in Regent Street, and an exhibition stand for Williams & Williams's 'Reliance' windows (1932), utilized only straight lines.

British Thompson Houston – whose stand Westwood and Emberton had designed at Wembley, commissioned one of a flush of Modern Movement shops in Regent Street. The windows were a simplified version of Allen–Liversidge; simple glass rectangles with the name, BTH Electric Refrigerators, in well-formed neon letters, forming an asymmetric composition with a band of indented reflective metal plates **(66)**. Stairs, crisply lighted, led downstairs to the showroom where a low display bench ran round the walls with a corresponding strip above, which housed a battery of round reflector lights. A central, glass-topped metal tube table and two metal tube cantilever chairs, probably by Thonet, the

Viennese firm whose London showroom was opened in the same year, were also lit by a central battery of reflector lights. The cabriole legs of the refrigerators were in sharp contrast to the four-square modernity of the setting (**67**). Williams & Williams's exhibition stand is an intricate facade, composed of golden section right-angles, both on the horizontal and on the vertical. There is a 'fire station' facade of huge doors; one stands open, a second is added to the front plane and stands forward into the no man's land of the threshold. Between these two elements the large rectangular space in the glass wall, the entrance proper, is further modulated by a free-standing cranked 'window' which has completely escaped from the primary wall plane (**68**).

In the Lancashire 'hundred' of Aumundernesse a peat-bottomed black pool was drained in the eighteenth century and became the playground of the industrial north of England. Here, at Blackpool, Emberton's town planning exercises at the Advertising Exhibitions took a new turn, and were applied to the intriguing exercises of Pleasure Beach layout. This is related to the traditional setting-out of fun fairs, at which rectangular and squarish side shows are used to form a pallisade, and round ones take up the roundish space in the centre. The South Shore Pleasure Beach is based on an American form; Amusement Parks were frequently sited at the ends of tramways, to provide magnets which would keep the trams in constant use. Such is the case at Blackpool, where the tramway still remains, and where for a long time the Pleasure Beach marked the South Shore terminus.

Emberton worked within the structure set up in the early 1900s, based on the American experience of the founders, John Outhwaite and William Bean.

Blackpool first became a watering-place in the middle of the eighteenth century when a few houses were built along the shoreline. The paving of the turnpike road from Preston in 1781 opened the way for travellers, and the railway, opened in 1846, did the same for the masses.

The masses began to go to Blackpool partly because of the railway, and partly because of the institution of the Wakes. Wakes are a North Country survival of the holidays held on the Eves of Saints days which became at the coming of industrialization an annual shut-down holiday. It is not economic to run a factory at less than full power, so whole factories went on holiday together. Not only whole factories; the system was so inclusive that whole towns shut down, and whole populations of towns were transported to Blackpool by train.

Alderman Bean, as he had become, understood the movement of crowds. He laid a boardwalk across the deep sand from the South Shore station, and the crowds walked to the Pleasure Beach. Sir Hiram Maxim's Flying Macine was the first ride to be built, designed by a pioneer of flying to interest the public in the sport. This was followed by the Big Dipper, Noah's Ark – a variation of the Crazy House – and the Virginian Reel.

In 1933 William Bean's son-in-law Leonard Thompson, who shared an accountant with Olympia's owners, briefed Emberton with his plans for rebuilding the Pleasure Beach 'in a unified modern design'. Almost immediately (construction happens fast at the Pleasure Beach) the new rides began to take form on the site (**69**). A miniature railway, the Fun House, the Jack and Jill slide, the Whip and the Grand National were followed by the (new) Virginian Reel and Noah's Ark, Speed Boats, 'Cuddle-Up', and Big Dipper Station. Of these, the most ambitious were the Fun House and the Grand National; the most charming, the Noah's Ark.

The Fun House (**70**) is a monument to physical movement. Though the plan is not the generator (the plan of the Grand National certainly is) – the Fun House is another architectural promenade – it is also very close to a traditional fairground tent, with a mechanical man, a robot tout with a dreadful laugh, to pull the crowds inside. The Fun House, strongly reminiscent of the 1933 Advertising Exhibition, has a rectangular, slotted facade, a tower on one side, and a curved corner with 'streamlining' on the other. The flat, white front is painted with clowns and 'Constructivist' men which animate in two dimensions; the name, in rocking letters, adds a third dimension (and amplified roars of laughter a fourth?). The way in leads through a turnstile, where the price of admission is paid, then up and round in a very narrow passage which immediately becomes dark. Suddenly the way passes behind the window slot between the painted clowns and, for the observer, real people are added to the nightmare composition. The passage continues until the traveller is quite disoriented, when he is expelled from the passage and onto a stage. But that is not the end. The path continues over a crazy collection of moving floors – Crash Bumper, Grating, Rocking Floor, Ice Walk, Drop Floor, Shaking Floor, Sahara Desert, Shuffleboard – and finally the traveller is released, free to join the graduates in two rows of cinema seats: Armchairs of the Elect.

The Fun House's 'architectural promenade' (Le Corbusier's term) leads through a succession of pleasing spaces, but not the magnificent succession of Diocletian's Palace or the lyrical progression of Villa Savoye. This is the pleasure which makes one laugh, the pleasure of surprise, the recognition of scientific phenomena ludicrously employed, the ridiculous pleasure of movement.

Wooden cut-out animals designed by Percy Metcalf stand outside the Noah's Ark Crazy House and watch the visitor's approach. Dangerously springy, wooden stepping-stones over water must be negotiated, making the Ark a real haven – but not a comfortable one. Floors suddenly drop, the brass handrail to the bridge is electrified, animals roar and scream, the promenade leads along dark, narrow passages down to a hold lit by ultra-violet light . . .

The Fun House and Noah's Ark came under the scrutiny of Tom Harrison and Charles Madge when, in 1938, they chose Blackpool (and Bolton) for a special study, 'Worktown', for one of the Mass Observation projects. Harrison and Madge, with the photographer Humphrey Spender (who had been a student at the Architectural Association in 1934), turned their anthropological attention onto our own culture, the 'savage civilization' of the Pleasure Beach. They observed three principal types of pleasure at the Pleasure Beach: making a fool of yourself; making a fool of others; doing the impossible.

The 'Grand National' (71) is not a steeplechase, but a car race. Three huge, round canopies mark the coming-together of the two diverging routes taken by the speedway cars – the unrealized Skegness speedway probably served as model for this. The gravity coasters race over a tortuous course at a maximum speed of 72 m.p.h. First one, then the other, takes the lead, but they arrive back at the disembarkation platform together, and are subjected to proper planning control – the departing riders are released by way of a tunnel which passes underneath the entrance steps. A cruciform tower signals the ride's name – again in the Emberton idiom of well-formed letters of coloured neon.

It is this theme, coloured light, which characterizes Emberton's next building, Simpson's of Piccadilly, thought by many to be his masterpiece (72). In contrast to the exuberance and playfulness of Blackpool, Simpson's has a gravity entirely in keeping with the elegance of London's Piccadilly.

In 1894, Simeon Simpson founded a clothing-manufacturing firm in Stoke Newington. His son Alexander, who introduced DAKS, self-supporting trousers which did away with the need for braces and waistcoats, wanted a West End showroom from which to challenge (in the Continental manner of ready-mades) Savile Row's traditional hold on tailoring.

At Simpson's, Emberton once more used a steel frame, but this time with a difference. The structural engineer, Felix Samuely of Helsby, Hamann and Samuely, whose structural design for Mendelsohn and Chermayeff's De la Warr

Pavilion was just being completed at Bexhill, Sussex, took another step forward and used, for the first time in London, a welded steel frame. Unhappily, this was too sophisticated a system for the administrators of London's Building Bye Laws. Samuely had proposed two welded plate girders, one at first and one at second floor level, restraining them, by completing the rectangle, at the supports. The London County Council requested that the two plate girders, which had already been fabricated, be freed of that end restraint (**73**). As by this action they were rendered incapable of carrying their intended load, the elegance of Samuely's structure was quite negated, and additional, simply supported, plate girders had to be inserted at every floor – and, the final indignity, had to be riveted. The welding machine, heavily booked, had by this time moved on.

The elevation of Simpson's is apparently simplicity itself, with five horizontal bands of windows, the top band set back with a canopied terrace in front, and the whole rectangle bordered by strong vertical bands of portland stone (at the requirement of the ground landlord) and bronze. But these 'simple' planes are canted, sloped and chamfered, behind and in front of the primary plane, giving endless variation in shade and shadow. The street level is clad in black granite, with a band of show-windows on either side of the entrance door, which has a cantilevered glass block canopy, spotlit from above. The concave, non-reflective glass in the windows is made to a patent registered in the mid Thirties. The north face, that most difficult of London orientations (there is a secondary entrance and facade at the back of the shop, in Jermyn Street), is entirely rescued by the inspired use of coloured light. Three neon tubes, red, blue and green, run in a moulded-bronze channel above each window strip. These tubes can be switched on singly, or in combination, to give floodlighting of red, blue, or green, red/blue, blue/green, or red/green (a vibrating brown), and red/blue/green (astonishingly in line with the theory of physics, a magical white).

The use of hidden sources of light is one of the most easily recognized details of Emberton's hand (**74, 75**). He also uses the characteristic plaster flange light baffle with slit openings for the introduction of air. When necessary it acts as a duct – at Simpson's ducts are required for vacuum, for cleaning and for the transport of cash – and its secondary use is to define a space, to indicate a route or, as at Blackpool Casino, to reflect the radiating structure. 'It is desirable', Emberton wrote, 'in schemes of indirect lighting that lamps of small wattage, say twenty watts, are placed about nine inches apart rather than lamps of higher wattage at greater intervals, otherwise an unevenly lighted surface will result. A scheme of this kind', he added, 'is somewhat extravagant in cost . . . and involves about

31

a thirty per cent increase in consumption, but as current gets cheaper so will the advantage of this smooth, diffuse, lighting become appreciated . . .'.[32]

Internally the building is divided into three parts, a division which met the requirements of fire regulations but is also successful architecturally (76). The whole is joined by the lovely, cream-coloured travertine stair which rises to one side of the central bay and is lit all the way up its height by a glass block bay-window and, at night, by a succession of pairs of spherical globes on a chrome rod (77) – a light fitting designed to animate the whole stairwell, worthy successor of a form devised by Eric Mendelsohn. Coloured handrails, on one side red/orange ('tango'), on the other cream, and white-painted fire-fighting equipment, completed the composition. In the sales areas Emberton also designed the fittings; long bands of cupboards fitted with doors which slide right round to the back, racks, for skirts or jackets, which run the whole width of the shop, and specialized shops: the cigar shop, faced with aromatic cedar, is still spoken of with nostalgia.

Some of the furniture was designed by Emberton, though he also used the work of other designers; leather and curved plywood armchairs and plywood tables by Alvar Aalto, PEL chairs, and rugs by Ashley Havinden and Natasha Kroll. A trousers table (78), metal-framed with a steam-curved ply top and a fascinating zig-zag cantilever, may have been designed by Emberton, who may also have designed the bar-stools and stools at the Royal Corinthian Yacht Club in the same style. The boardroom and staff lounge furniture is by Emberton, part of a series that was made for him by Bath Cabinet Makers, who also made cupboards, a dressing table, desk and dining table for his own house. All were in the simplest of shapes, veneered in bird's eye maple, elm or sycamore.

In 1935, Laslo Moholy Nagy and Gyorgy Kepes, refugees from Nazi Germany, arrived in England to take up their shared positions as Art Directors at Simpson's, responsible for display and window design. Moholy Nagy, who had been teaching on the theme of coloured light at the Bauhaus, was introduced to Simpson by Ashley Havinden who handled Simpson's advertising at Crawford's Advertising Agency. 'The success of the venture', wrote Moholy's wife Sybil, 'depended on unimpeachable taste, which would quell any objections to cheapness and vulgarity . . . here was Moholy's chance to translate his knowledge of light and colour into reality . . .'.[33]

What could have become a fertile partnership between architect and designer failed to transpire, and each kept strictly to his own brief. Certainly since the Allen–Liversidge shop, and possibly since the rumoured pavilion in Paris of 1925, 'very small, very prettily lit', Emberton had made use of coloured light. He

32

used it in his Regent Street shops, BTH Refrigerators and Ardath, and with greatest effect at Universal House, where the thin, careful proportions of the neon lettering he acknowledged as having been learned from the Netherlands Pavilion at the Antwerp Exhibition (1930, H. Th. Wijdeveld) (79). 'It has only recently been recognized that lettering itself can form a very adequate decoration for the exterior of the building. This was illustrated in a most exquisite manner by the Dutch pavilion at the Antwerp Exhibition.'[34] It is most likely that Emberton, as an experienced hand at exhibition design, is speaking at first hand of Wijdeveld's pavilion, and that the visit to Holland referred to in *Den Acht en Opbouw* took place at this time.

An account of Simpson's published in the Netherlands is cautiously complimentary: 'We cannot say that this building is an example of functional architecture. If we set it beside a single example of functional architecture from our own country – the Hilversum hotel of J. Duiker [80] or A. Boeken's Tennis Hall in Amsterdam, we shall see an important difference . . . Simpson's shop has neither the constructional principles nor the elegance and playfulness that characterize Duiker's hotel – but for England this is not the point. It is more important to recognise this building as a symptom of "l'Esprit Nouveau".'[35] No mean epithet for a British building at this time, but still parsimonious. Simpson's does have elegance, and Samuely's structural design, even with the over-cautious interference of the LCC, establishes this elegance in the facade. The stylishness of the 1930s has persisted, so that Simpson's in the 1980s is a classic.

Simpson's, and a shop for the chemist chain Timothy White's in Southsea, Hampshire, were Emberton's contribution to the second exhibition of Modern Architecture held at the Museum of Modern Art, New York: 'Modern Architecture in England – 1937'.

Timothy White's (1934) (81) resembles Universal House, with its glass wall ornamented by coloured neon letters and the chemist's traditional bottle symbol. In its plan it resembles Simpson's, the Ardath shop, and the HMV shop (1939, Oxford Street, London). This plan uses the curving shapes of counters to direct customers through the shopkeeper's display. The floor space is like a lake, through which the customer is floated, past inviting, rounded islands to his destination, and then efficiently returned to the street. The rough-cast glass of the facade is held in place by galvanized steel strips painted battleship grey. The lettering is in bent aluminium tube and the bottle symbol is in aluminium tube and neon.

The year 1934 saw the completion of two other projects: two blocks of 'philanthropic housing' in Stepney, East London – Chapman House and Turnour House – and a physiotherapy clinic, the Alfred Eicholz clinic for the Royal National Institute for the Blind, in Portland Place, London W1.

Between 1926 and 1951 Emberton designed only three houses, the Weybridge house, a house for his sister in Audley, Staffordshire (1939), and the prototype for a mass-produced steel house; and two blocks of flats, Chapman House and Turnour House. After 1951, with the exception of renovations to the Theatre Royal, Drury Lane, after bomb damage, he designed *only* flats. His earliest flats, artisans' dwellings for the Chapman Development Trust, were intended to give the best accommodation possible under the current building conditions for people who could afford from sixteen shillings to £1 a week in rent.

Chapman House (**82**) is an 'L'-shaped block, four storeys high, with the fourth storey, which has a flat roof, set back to give a balcony fenced with metal tube and diamond mesh. The same mesh encloses a roof-top play area at one end. The flats are reached by balconies which connect with a detached, round-ended stair which also houses a rubbish chute. Lifting hooks contribute to a Dutch look, which is continued by the extreme compactness of the space inside the flats. The corner flat has an entrance lobby off which a bathroom, a living room, a bedroom and a large cupboard open. The kitchen is an alcove off the living room and helps to form a second alcove which is curtained off as a bedroom. The third and fourth bedrooms also open out of the living room. On the outside face the corner window, which wraps around the corner, is no more than a bedroom window – one would have hoped that this big window would somehow have been incorporated into the living room. The material is reinforced concrete, painted pale grey, with green metal windows. Turnour House (**83, 84**), a few streets away, is an improved version of the same thing, a simple block, from which the living-room windows are pulled forward to provide modelling to the front. There is a small balcony generally, and a good-sized balcony for the fourth floor. At the back a concrete stair, as at Chapman House, gives access to 'street balconies'. The same Crittal's metal windows are used, as is the same diamond mesh, the same grey-washed stucco and green paint. T. P. Bennet is named as a consultant, and there is a curious reciprocation, since Bennet names Emberton consultant for *his* up-market flats, Dorset House, in Marylebone Road. Emberton's part there was the elevation, which was, said Bennet in 1975, 'rather in advance of the architectural thought of its time'. It did not meet with the approval of the Board, so 'we merely put it on the files.'

The Alfred Eicholz clinic (1934) is an interior scheme. One cannot imagine a better choice of architect for the blind – the logical flow of the circulation, rounded corners which will not bark the shins of the stranger, efficient lighting and the use of strong colour on light switches and handrails, are exactly what is needed, particularly for those with residual sight. To the connoisseur of Emberton's interiors the scheme exudes the usual sense of efficient and cheerful repose.

The Olympia Garage, finished in 1936, is a rigorous exercise in logical form. The ground floor, which acts as a Classical podium, follows the line of the street, but the four upper floors curve in a manner similar to Mendelsohn's Schocken store at Chemnitz, although here the curve rises, following the easy spiral of the ramp. The distinction between the straight and the curved is further marked by the use of black brick for the podium and buff brick for the upper part. The building was much admired for its functionalism, the curve dictated by the turning circle of a climbing car, and (unusual for Emberton) the lack of any kind of ornament.

If there is uncertainty as to whether Emberton participated in the Paris Exhibition of 1925, there is no doubt of his presence at the 1937 exhibition. A brochure, apparently unpublished, shows photographs of a pavilion for Lever Bros (**85, 86**) (advertising 'Soleil', the French version of Sunlight Soap). The photographs show an exhibition pavilion the size of a large cinema. A huge, three-storey glass wall reminds us of Universal House and Timothy White's, but the applied ornament, of which there is much, is anachronistic. The glass wall, against the inside of which an escalator seems to move, is bounded on one side by a huge entrance pylon, and on the other side by a smaller one – though still large. An enclosing wall surrounds a large interior space in which French provincial laundry-maids demonstrate 'Soleil' soap. Minor entrances are punched into the wall, each one marked by gigantic piers sculpted in low relief, and the wall itself is banded and crocketed in a manner which Emberton had not employed since 1927. Although it subscribes to the prevailing taste of the exhibition, the pavilion is surprisingly out of keeping for a design which must be set between Simpson's and Blackpool Casino.

The Glasgow International Exhibition of 1938 reunited Emberton and Thomas Tait for the first time since they had worked together on Adelaide House in the early Twenties. Tait had been appointed by his native city as architect to the exhibition, which was held in Bellahouston Park, and was particularly remarkable for what has become known as 'Tait's Tower'. This was essentially the landmark for the exhibition, in the same way that Emberton used towers in his Pleasure Beach rides, and it has a marked resemblance to Jan Wils's tower at the Amsterdam Stadium.

The central point of the exhibition was the Garden Club, a large, low building like a huge garden pavilion, which accommodated restaurants, lounges and meeting places, and which sprawled, in plan a modified C scroll, at the head of an enormous flight of shallow steps. The exhibition owed much in design to the ground broken by Gunnur Asplund, at his Stockholm Exhibition of 1930. Asplund, a follower of Le Corbusier, had taken his style and made it lighter and more cheerful, more suitable for a Scandinavian summer. Tait too employed this cheerful airiness, although something of Asplund's quality is lost. Emberton's building at Glasgow, the British Railways Pavilion (**87**), also seems to owe something to Asplund, as does his Pleasure Beach work, but it is tightly controlled and in the line of development both of his version of the architectural promenade and of his work on the massing and conjoining of circular forms. It consists of an entrance terrace which leads forward to a circular concourse, and left to a model railway track wrapped round offices and an exhibition of railway carriage interiors. The curved wall of the offices is ornamented with 'drawings' in square-section black wire, raised just off the surface. This device was used as a room decoration by Oscar Schlemmer at the Bauhaus, and recently had been introduced to England by Marcel Breuer at Heal's 'Seven Architects' exhibition in 1936. Externally the disparate elements are resolved into a tall concrete and glass cylinder with full-height, punched-out windows and accretions of canopies, reminiscent of the Blackpool Grand National, and a thin, asymmetrically placed tower. The plan, like that of Blackpool Casino, which followed in 1939, and that of some of the Pleasure Beach rides, has a spinning quality; but the elevation is resolved and obviously derives – as did the exterior form of the stair tower at the Casino, which must have been on the drawing board at the same time – from Mendelsohn and Chermayeff's De La Warr pavilion at Bexhill (1936) (**88**).

Emberton's HMV (His Master's Voice) shop in Oxford Street (1939) (**89**) followed the British Rail Pavilion. Although with exactly the same orientation as Simpson's – a North-facing London street – Emberton's approach here is slightly different. Instead of using electric light he uses daylight. The elevation is a simple, well-proportioned rectangle, in which three horizontal bands of glass blocks are set with casement windows. Instead of advertisement by coloured light, he uses blatant advertisement, like the chemist's bottle at Timothy White's; the HMV dog and gramophone take up the whole of one storey. A windowless wall is the internal result, and this is utilized for acoustically treated gramophone listening cubicles. Oxford Street did not have then (any more than it has today, even at the Marble Arch end) anything like the same elegance as Piccadilly. Accordingly, Emberton dispenses with the dignified central entrance of Simpson's. He curves and swings the entrance glass, bringing the goods into the street and the customer into the shop in one move. Once inside, the swinging curves are continued in the counter lines in an inside-out version of the British Railways Pavilion.

The central space is again defined by the flowing line of the counters, which themselves follow the space that remains when offices and stores have been inserted against the outer walls. The space sweeps from counter to counter and, finally, up and down the stairs – which are completely internal, unmarked on the elevation. The stairway, like the stairway at the Casino, is a continuous ample spiral in reinforced concrete but, unlike the Casino stair which is cantilevered from a huge central column, this stair cantilevers off the enclosing wall, so that it has an open central well. Here, as if there had been enough twisting, the light fitting is rigorously straight and thin. Instead of the paired globes of Simpson's, groups of nine-inch long tubes are clustered on a similar chromed rod (**90**).

It is curious that in a self-consciously modern wireless and gramophone shop, so little was made of the essential radio receiver tower. The tower was visually minimal, and made little contribution to the composition. Today it has disappeared completely, together with the curving counters and the original dog and gramophone symbol on the front elevation.

Emberton's Audley house for his sister Dorothy quietly states its designer's predilections (**91**). It shows its relationship to the Westwood and Emberton house of 1927 by its timber shingle roof, though the plan here is far simpler. On the front elevation Emberton uses the staircase window to provide a vertical balance to the horizontal rectangles of the bedroom windows. The front porch is turned away from the garage entrance and has connotations of both timber cabins and Dutch De Stijl detailing.

Emberton's use of colour is always personal and always admirable. 'I am enclosing a tile' he wrote to his sister. 'It seems to me an extraordinarily nice colour.' This colour, a vibrant cornelian red, must have been his favourite. He used it as a fine line in the bathroom tiles at Audley, in the stairs handrail at the Casino, where it was called 'tomato' and at Simpson's, where it was called 'tango'. Also at Audley, between the dark shadow of the overhanging eaves and the dark brown of the weatherboarding, he seems to have used a strong emerald green on the metal windows and rainwater gutters. The plan is surprising in a house for a country housewife. One enters by the porch to a small hall with a tiny cloakroom under the stair, which is cranked round a square well. From the hall one may enter the kitchen ahead, or the living room to the left. The living room takes up the whole of one side of the house. Into the kitchen a back door opens via pantries and stores, and from the kitchen, a door and a serving hatch open into a small dining room. This means that the kitchen has doors on three walls, and is virtually a pass-through space into which is fitted a central table, a stove and a sink – nothing had been learned from the many experimental kitchens of this time (**92**).

Although, in common with many Modern architects of the 1930s, Emberton thought it was impossible to design with an aesthetic aim in mind, that beauty would come of itself born of efficiency, he nevertheless continuously employed some sort of 'bible' – a collection of source writings on the ethics and aesthetics of form and proportion. Allan Ure, remembering Emberton's reading of the 1920s, could recall Jay Hambidge's *Dynamic Form*, Lund's *Ad Quadratum*, Coleman's *Nature's Harmonic Unity*, and Theodore Cook's *The Curves of Life*.

'*The Modulor*[36] was always lying on his desk', said Carl-Ludwig Franck, recalling the 1950s – but later corrected himself: 'if it was, it was only to be put aside the next day. He was always on to something else'.[37]

Theodore Cook's study of spiral forms grew out of his study of the architecture of Northern France. The question arose of the authorship of the left-handed spiral stair at the Chateau of Blois, attributed to a left-handed man, Leonardo da Vinci. Cook remained fascinated by the subject, and *The Curves of Life*[38] is the result.

The Curves of Life seems to have been put aside for nearly ten years. Emberton had received it in 1924 from the Secretary of the British Electrical and Allied Manufacturers' Association (whose acquaintance demonstrates Emberton's serious attitude to electricity) but he does not seem to have used it until 1933, when he started work at Blackpool. The Grand National's plan is the result of the form of the racecourses, but the form of the racecourses is derived from Cook.

Emberton never had an architectural library, but his wife still has his copy of *The Curves of Life* on her bookself – and a pencil line has been added to the diagram of the growth of a spiral (**93**). The plan of Blackpool Casino is based on this.

At the outbreak of war in 1939, two more 'casinos' were being planned, one at Southport and one at Morecambe. If Blackpool Casino's plan represents stage 1 in the growth of a spiral, these two others represent stage 2 and stage 3. The first design for the Casino was a two-storey building, circular in shape, the upper storey slightly set back. The white concrete band separating the windows drops to ground level and is brought forward to support a banded entrance canopy. Secondary entrances, also framed in concrete, are set round the perimeter. The squat, double saucer has its own tall tower – an over-high funnel, joined by fins to an even taller flat plane. A drawing of this shows elegant people, with few children, but many splendid motor cars. The towers of the Grand National and the Big Dipper station in the background form, with the Casino, a 'Brave New World' (**94**).

The final design put more emphasis on the stair tower, which becomes a glass cylinder apparently about to be thrown off by the implied spin of the greater volume. The ornamental tower is moved, and becomes an engaging reinforced concrete corkscrew which marks the entrance, over which an advertisement grid and a wheel invite comparison with pit-head machinery. This must be deliberate, in that it replaces the less apposite funnel, and must be seen as a compliment to holidaying miners (**95**).

Soon after the building was completed a third floor was added, really a wind-screen for the sunbathing and gymnastics deck. Centrifugal rooflets mark each column (a far cry from Adelaide House) and form small external sun parlours which keep up a steady rhythm round the roofline (**96**).

The Casino lies on a subsoil of silting sand, and rests on an upturned tray of reinforced concrete (**97**). A system of radiating beams with cantilevered and tapered ends and concentric rings of columns provides a skeleton. The reinforced concrete was designed by 'Truscon', The Trussed Concrete and Steel Co.; no engineer is named. Window glass set in thin, reinforced-concrete panels forms the skin. These facing panels, designed and made in Holland by Schokbeton N.V., were delivered to Blackpool by water on barges. The stair tower like the stair tower of Simpson's is of glass and concrete, this time much larger, vertically placed rectangular panes are set directly into grooves in the pre-cast panels (**98**). Single or double grooves allow for single or double glazing, according to exposure. The stair, a continuous spiral, cantilevers off a central column with handrails – as at Simpson's, one cream, one 'tomato' (**99**).

The interior was almost completely taken up by restaurants (**100–102**). The Promenade entrance led directly to a small, elegant First Class restaurant, and to the Banqueting Room on the first floor. The main entrance served the Main Restaurant, and the Pleasure Beach entrance, the Soda Fountain and Quick Lunch

Bar – service counters with stools radiated from the central kitchen core into the segment-shaped space. The Main Restaurant was equipped with a stage and a rising floor, and all the restaurants could expand or contract, sliding screens roll away in tracks to fold completely away in sidings.

The Banqueting Room, which could seat a thousand people (a trainload from Manchester) had a raised terrace on the perimeter, and a balcony that ran round the seaward facing side of the building. Offices and stores took up the landward side. The colour-scheme was broken white with grey-painted metalwork, 'tomato' red columns and cream terrazzo floors.

The building has recently been modernized and repaired. The pre-cast concrete skin has been renovated and painted white, but the hard marble-like skin with its satisfying rounded contours has been sacrificed. Unlike the Royal Corinthian Yacht Club, which is maintained like a boat, the Casino had been neglected, particularly, though understandably, during the war years. In one place the stylishness of the Thirties still survives, though perhaps not for long, in the owner's flat on the roof. A steep, narrow, ply-veneered staircase arrives at a landing which joins kitchen and apartment proper. The kitchen is only an after-thought, as food was intended to be delivered from the central kitchen. One enters the living room, which is connected by a corridor on the same curve as the building to a bathroom and two bedrooms. All the rooms are panelled and fitted with furniture veneered in burr maple, with cream plastic handles (**103**). Dressing tables and wardrobes are birds-eye-maple faced, with glass shelves, mirrors, and batteries of thin cream handles. Bathroom and toilet are lined in cream and green glass. Doors too are veneered, as is the whole corridor. Door handles are a good blue green. A sofa has a built-in ashtray, shelf and telephone table, and a circular dining table is wired with service bell-pushes under the top.

Director Ken Russell planned to film his *Valentino* here, though the 'ship's stair' proved too narrow to take the cameras. But he was right to select this 'set' for *Valentino* – the whole simple and consistently designed entity glows with the gold of maple, a worthy reminder of the Casino in its heyday, the short summer of 1939. The Dutch press was not available to comment on the successor to Simpson's, nor, for that matter was much of the British press; but there is little doubt that here were to be found the inventive structural principles, the informed playfulness admired by Emberton, as well as by his critics of *Den Acht en Opbouw*, in the work of the Dutch avant garde.

Summing up Emberton's work in 1939, C. H. Reilly concluded with a note on the Casino. Restaurants, banqueting rooms, bars and games rooms were there, but no ballroom; and dancing is in the spirit of the building. Blackpool Corporation would be well advised to hand over to Emberton the design of the whole town: 'especially, let him design their famous, but really rather infamous, illuminations'.[39]

Emberton and Leonard Thompson animated the Pleasure Beach in a unified and coherent modern idiom. Their energy spread over the whole of the Pleasure Beach, encompassing advertising, menus, and decorations in the bars and restaurants. They travelled widely, to Disneyland and Luna Park, and to Brussels, where they built a Funfair in 1930 at the Brussels International Exhibition. 'Advertising plan needed based on Angol Park, Budapest. Suggest Miss Lockey should see what she can do', runs a note from Thompson to Emberton.[40]

Joan Lockey and Margaret Blundell, together with Percy Metcalf and Tom Purvis, were called upon to provide work which ranged from a stylized elevation of the Casino to advertisements for skating, wrestling and a boat club, restaurant decorations based on the Flying Machine of Sir Hiram Maxim, the Noah's Ark, and the Helter Skelter (104–113). A plan and elevation of a Wild Mouse has notes appended: 'Nose, solid rubber, will act as buffer' and 'a knot in his tail would make any mouse wild' (114).

Is this architectural design? The total art work, the *gesamtkunstwerk*, of the Pleasure Beach went almost unnoticed. Even the marble-like finish to Schokbeton's concrete did not receive its due acclaim, and by the time post-war shortages had relaxed enough to allow such expert design once more, this example had been forgotten. One celebrated couple did make a report. Hugh and Margaret Casson visited the Casino and wrote an account in *Architectural Review*,[41] but they missed many opportunities. Journalists of the stature of *Den Acht en Opbouw* were needed, and they could not be there.

During the 1939–45 war, Emberton was still applying his principle that 'every problem has its logical solution', but the stringencies of war reduced the possibilities for the discovery that a preferred functional element was also ornamental. In 1931 he had said that architecture's greatest hope lay in the need for stringent economy, pointing to the spare beauty of the outright winner of the Schneider Trophy (115). 'This could not have been designed aesthetically, yet it is one of the most exquisite forms man has produced, and could compare with nature's own structures. Nature seems to decree that any job well done should have a seemly appearance.'[42] The Spitfire and the Junkers 88 may have had the same exquisite forms as the Schneider Trophy-winning seaplane, but Emberton's own wartime work did not please him. After the war, when he moved from London to Brighton, he ordered a rubbish skip, and the war work disappeared into it.

During the early post-war years he worked on hostels for mine workers – the so called Bevin Boys – and at the Ministry of Works. He wrote to Leonard Thompson that he had met with the four Ministers concerned with housing, and had given them a lecture on flats. The result seems to have been the prototype for a steel house. 'The steel house was designed at the end of the war (1949), when I was acting consultant at the Ministry of Works, with the intention of using machine tools which had been acquired for the construction of the Portal Temporary One Storey House [which was used during and immediately after the war for temporary housing]. The prototype had hardly been completed when it was found that there was no steel available.'[43]

In some ways this house (116) is based on the Casino flat which, in its turn, was an improvement on the Audley house. The Audley house is so underprovided with cupboards, and has such an inconvenient kitchen, in contrast to both the Casino flat and the steel house, that it would seem that this is a result of the demands of the client. The design of the steel house, planned to utilize surplus steel, was agreed with the Ministry of Health, and the technical details were developed under Emberton's supervision at the Ministry of Supply. But before it could go into production, steel became unavailable and the project was shelved. At the time, each house would have cost £1250 and would have taken eleven men one week to erect. The prototype was constructed by a car-body firm, Briggs Bodies of Dagenham, in Essex, and the house makes use of the properties of construction suitable to car-manufacturing plant. The external walls are formed of a pressed-steel outer skin of panels, each measuring 3 ft 6 ins. by 8 ft, filled with aereated concrete and faced on the inside with hardboard. These panels were loadbearing and carried the weight of both floor and roof. All external panels were identical in form, and the units could be assembled to produce houses of various sizes. The roof was also formed from 3 ft 6 ins. panels, with insulation similar to that of the walls, and was curved with the object of stiffening the light gauge pressed-steel external facing. The plan is for efficient, semi-detached houses, a double skin between them, and separated on the second side by a single-storey addition housing a large store, toilet, and fuel store. The front door leads to a large hall with a pram space and gives entrance to the living room, kitchen ahead, and the stairs on one side. The kitchen has a fair-sized run of work-top, with a two-sided cupboard into the dining extension of the living room. Upstairs, a cupboard/partition separates the bedrooms (117, 118).

42

The pressed steel was treated to resist rust and painted with textured paint. 'How can we support our roses?' joked the prospective tenants. 'You will have to weld them on', answered Emberton, but tackled the question with characteristic efficiency. He added two welded-on bars with strings between them, and bracketed-on, rounded window boxes – recognized the necessity and turned it into ornament. The addition (to the prototype) of a sun-blind tacitly suggests a brighter future and the need for shade.

Emberton completed a factory in 1949 for the Easiwork company, producers of kitchen machines, for which Raymond McGrath had designed a showroom in Regent Street, almost next door to Emberton's two shops. The factory was constructed from pre-fabricated reinforced-concrete sections, small enough for easy transportation, bolted together on site to form 'Y'-shaped beams, and with patent glazing on the steep slope – a new form of North-light roof (119). Efficient and cheap to maintain, the building claimed little for the architect.

The blocks of flats which, from this point, complete Emberton's work, are big, each taller than the last, but one has the feeling that the same amount of spirit has to stretch to animate larger and larger buildings. Emberton was receiving commissions from the London Borough of Finsbury, which became available following the dissolution of the Tecton partnership, the Borough's previous architect, but there is a feeling of desolation present in the work which seemed to pervade architecture in general at that time. Potentially the most interesting project was the 1951 Festival of Britain, though this was severely restricted by post-war austerities. Yet, due to illness, Emberton would not have been unable to contribute to the event, for which his skill at turning the need for stringency to the best effect made him uniquely qualified.

The Finsbury work consists of a six-storey block of flats – Stuart Mill House, Killick Street, N1 (1951) (120), and two housing estates, one completed by Emberton's partners, Carl-Ludwig Franck and Tim Tardrew.

Stuart Mill House is simple and neat. A brick volume, banded at floor level and fronted with the horizontal strips of the entrance balconies, a porch marks the asymmetrical entrance and the line of the porch is carried up the whole front by a glass screen. Balancing this, at the top floor, an escape stair breaks free of the balconies and drops one floor. Emberton reasserts his delight in making necessity – a fire regulation – become ornamental.

The Stafford Cripps Estate consists of three Y-shaped blocks of flats and a commercial block, in a carefully considered communal garden – in practice virtually unused. The great failure of the scheme is the absence of an axis. The three winged forms are so non-directional, it is difficult to find the way in and, because there is no 'back', once found, the way in seems inevitably to be between rubbish containers.

But there are some virtues. The entrance porches are cranked towards the visitor, and neatly lit (**121**). Balconies are equipped with a timber shelf against which the tenant is invited to lean (**122**), and there are some structural innovations – the floors are of four-inch thick reinforced concrete. The location is bad – near two major city roads, and well away from any green space – and the 'garden' does not succeed in alleviating this.

Nor does the garden at Brunswick Close. The Brunswick Estate consists of three fourteen-storey slab blocks, each with a second wing at ground level and a stair/lift tower at right-angles to each slab. The floor slab is again of four-inch concrete, and once more Emberton uses the 'decorative' device of special escape stairs. But the high, dark towers are a signal of the failure of tall flats. Flats in the sky were new, and few had lived in them. They were a 'solution' to ribbon development which proved to be no solution at all.

Emberton's last enthusiasm was for the rebuilding of the devastated area around St Paul's Cathedral. One block of the Stafford Cripps Estate type was used as a model for a whole landscape built over with three-pronged towers (**123**) – straight out of Le Corbusier's Radiant City, but with an unmistakable relationship to Duiker's Gooiland Hotel. A similar scheme was proposed for the Paternoster site at St Paul's. Carl-Ludwig Franck's perspective shows St Paul's set majestically among towers, each one differently modelled at the top, in the best New York skyscraper tradition (**124**).

At a meeting of the Architecture Club (of which the second president had been Sir Lawrence Weaver, and which had entertained, in Emberton's time, Frank Lloyd Wright, Berlage and Duiker) held at Simpson's Restaurant in the Strand in November 1956, supper was followed by a debate on the proposition 'that St Paul's be given a picturesque and not a Classical setting'. Was it intended to provoke the Modernist? It provoked Emberton (**125**), attending the dinner with his daughter Jocelyn, and he gave his speech on the side of the angels. The report in *The Architect's Journal* is terse: 'The debate was opened by Sir William Holford and Sir Giles Gilbert Scott and continued by G. A. Jellicoe, Peter Smithson, A. S. G. Butler, Dr Thomas Sharp, H. S. Goodhart Rendell, Sir Patrick Abercrombie, Lieut. Col. Cart Lafontaine, Mr Joseph Emberton and Mr Cyril

Carter. Unhappily Mr Emberton was taken fatally ill after making his speech.'[44]

'His tastes and opinions were as I recall rather simple', wrote Serge Chermayeff. 'He liked fast cars and picnics – so did we. Like us, he and his wife preferred friends to colleagues to relax with – Emberton had little interest in Modern Art – then emerging in England. Most of our intimate friends were, per contra, among artists and intellectuals – I recall him as an architect exclusively working in that medium. He was not an intellectual.'[45]

Chermayeff's assessment of Emberton's tastes and opinions as 'simple' seems to be born out by Emberton's own writings, but on occasion he attains the Roman quality of 'simplicitas' – plainness, straightness of grain. His admiration for the 'one big simple idea' of Selfridges, so similar to that of Burnet's North Gallery of the British Museum, is of this sort; no trivial simplicity.

On the rare occasions on which he does address Modern Art, his attitude is, however, probably over-simple, reflecting both an exclusively architectural position and the Modernist architect's dogmatic attitude to ornament. 'We shall learn that portraits soon become anachronisms – the clothes of fifty or a hundred years ago become of more interest than the purpose of the statues. These will be symbolical, and not in the uneasy transitional stage of Mr Epstein who still clings to recognisably human forms. Nor will such ornaments be set up on buildings whose purpose has nothing to do with the subject of the sculpture, like groups of Night and Day on the headquarters of London's Underground.'[46]

But he does not hold to this view with rigour, probably rightly so. He does not seem to have needed to clear his palate with Louis Sullivan's total ban on ornament.[47] His own taste for simplicity seems to have given him a capacity to continue to use ornament of an appropriately modern derivation.

His dislike of the reshuffled forms of Edwardian architecture did not prevent him, on occasion, from reshuffling Modernist forms; in the house at Weybridge, and at Olympia, he inexplicably contributed to the 'ethical' counter-arguments surrounding the use or misuse of reinforced concrete.

In his article in the *Evening News*, written as the architect of the new Olympia, he seems temporarily to have allowed himself to forget that the structure is of brick and steel. 'We are still labouring', he lectured, 'under the misconception that buildings should be treated as if they were stone. The day of stone is past: marble is no longer a building material. Let us forget the Renaissance . . . and concentrate on our modern building material, which is reinforced concrete.' Sir Reginald Blomfield, 'Hammer of the Modernists', did not miss this, and in a radio programme, 'Is Modern Architecture on the Right Track?',[48] he questioned nine architects.

Blomfield introduced the programme by putting his own position: 'Though our Modernist may prefer "Olympia" to the Parthenon . . . who is going to be moved, except to resentment, by buildings such as Herr Mendelsohn produces in Germany or M. Corbusier in France, or by buildings of steel and brick [Olympia?] that purport to be made of concrete, buildings cased in steel and glass [Universal House?] that appear to follow no principle but that of contradicting anything that has ever been done before?'

Emberton, among the nine, did not answer the challenge, but when his turn came, he began by examining the use of 'Modern'. Interestingly he assigned to it its general meaning, and not its meaning as a style label. He took it to mean 'what is built today', and in his terms, this includes South Africa House in Trafalgar Square, and the Shell Building next to the Adelphi site. These two, he said, are probably not on the right track – 'On the other hand, if the expression is limited to those new forms, such as the Van Nelle Factory, Rotterdam, which have been developed in Germany, France and Holland, the answer is very definitely "yes". Architecture is not a matter of aesthetics. It is a matter of reason. Architecture should be the servant of man, and not man the servant of architectural tradition.' He argued that the heavy and wide Norman pier was replaced by the more slender Gothic column, and that the cause of this was an increased knowledge in the bearing capacity of stone – 'Why, therefore', he concluded, 'should we not accept the more attenuated form of a steel or reinforced-concrete column?' He cited the familiar concepts from *Vers une Architecture*, but added, 'I believe that the only way to achieve good architecture is to employ the most appropriate materials which scientific development has produced in providing such buildings as will give the utmost service to man without any aesthetic prejudice whatever – "To follow the argument wherever it may lead".' This quotation from Plato, and the ideas surrounding it, seem to hark back to his student days at the Kensington College of Art. Lethaby used the same phrase in a series of articles entitled 'A National Architecture' when he recommends 'Playing the game of variation, going where the argument leads and seeking to exhaust the possibilities of combination'.[49] Lethaby also considered that brick, rubble and mud (poured concrete?) are all part of the same construction system: 'articulation in carpentry, blockage in masonry, concretion in mud, rubble and brick . . . concrete should be frankly used. If blocks are better for constructive reasons than a continuous mass then use blocks by all means, but do not imitate a stone. The surfaces should be finished with white colour wash.'[50] This common-sense view seems to have been absorbed by Emberton and may account for his lack of dogmatism at Olympia. On the other hand it may be argued that the steel rods in reinforced concrete give rise to quite different structural behaviour, possibly akin to that of timber, and probably necessitating an additional category in Lethaby's table.

Emberton's claim that he learned nothing at the Kensington College of Art must be treated with caution, as must his aversion to 'aesthetics'. As with many modern architects, what he said must be matched against what he did. What he *said* was that 'beauty will come, it is born of efficiency, it is God's reward for virtue – in architecture anyhow.'[51] What he *did* was to interpret 'efficiency' and 'virtue' in a predominantly architectural way. In the same newspaper article he discussed the appropriateness of the Schneider Trophy itself, contrasted with that of the winner of the trophy, the Royal Aero Club's seaplane SD6. The form of the trophy, an Art Nouveau flurry of Nereids and waves, represents, he said man's representation of flight at 300 m.p.h. The seaplane, by contrast, is God's idea of the event – 'the form of the machine was forced upon the engineers by nature.'

What endures is Emberton's brand of Functionalism, his search for roots, a living tradition in which to work, and the consequences of this. When the new architectural impulse came from the continent in the late 1920s, Emberton was already at work. Until he had roots, in the tradition of Alexander Thomson, John Burnet, Thomas Tait and the new Dutch avant-garde, he only knew what he did not accept – the reshuffling of antique forms. Once he had a tradition in which to work, the previously undigested teaching of Lethaby seems to have become accessible. The logic and reason he found whilst in the artillery during the First World War could be added to the new Functionalism which was the natural antidote to Edwardian Revivalist styles. But Functionalism is not a creed one can rely on. There are long moments when the architect is not incontrovertibly informed of the correct mode of action. Even when one follows the argument, the form is not necessarily forced upon the architect by nature. As such times the architect is thrown back on his own efficiency, his own virtue.

Emberton was equal to this; the evidence of his architectural benevolence is consistent and clear.

Notes

1. H. S. Goodhart Rendell, 'Ricardo and Pite', *The Architect and Building News*, 6 December 1935.
2. Le Corbusier, *Vers une Architecture*, Paris 1923.
3. W. R. Lethaby, *Architecture*, London 1911.
4. C. H. Reilly, 'Some Younger Architects of Today', *Building*, August 1931.
5. Richard Cork, *Vorticism*, London 1976, vol. I, p. 49.
6. C. H. Reilly, 'The Training of Architects', *University Review*, July 1905.
7. C. H. Reilly, *Building*, August 1931.
8. Ibid.
9. Allan Ure, conversation with the author, 1976.
10. Sir Lawrence Weaver, *Architectural Review*, 1924, p. 226.
11. Sir Lawrence Weaver, *Exhibitions and the Art of Display*, London 1925.
12. Kathleen Emberton, conversation with the author, 1973.
13. Joseph Emberton, 'Modern Store Design', *Specification 34*, 1932.
14. Sir Nikolaus Pevsner, *The Buildings of England: London*, London 1952, vol. 2, p. 535.
15. R. H. Pearson, conversation with the author, 1975.
16. *Architectural Association Journal*, June 1929.
17. *Evening News*, 18 September 1929.
18. Eric Mendelsohn, *Bauen und Skizzen*, 1924. English translation: *Structures and Sketches*, London 1929.
19. Frederick Towndrow, *Building*, October 1929, p. 462.
20. C. H. Reilly, *Building*, August 1931.
21. Aquatint and drypoint. Collection of Mrs Emberton.
22. Phorpres Bricks. Advertisement widely published in the architectural press, 1929.
23. *Architectural Association Journal*, June 1929.
24. *Modern Architecture in England*. Museum of Modern Art, New York 1937.
25. *Den Acht en Opbouw* 1934, p. 101.
26. Cyril J. Goodman, 'A New Clubhouse', in *One Hundred Years of Amateur Yachting 1872–1972*, Royal Corinthian Yacht Club 1972.
27. Dated 2 December 1929. Heinz collection, RIBA.
28. *Boukundig Werkblad Architectura*, 12 March 1932.
29. John Ruskin, 'The Lamp of Truth. *Aphorism 15*: Cast-Iron Ornamentation Barbarous', from *The Seven Lamps of Architecture*, London 1849.
30. Raymond McGrath, *Glass in Architecture and Decoration*, London 1937.
31. *The Architect and Building News*, 21 August 1931.
32. Joseph Emberton, 'Modern Store Design', *Specification 34*, 1932.
33. Sybil Moholy Nagy, *Experiment in Totality*, New York 1950.
34. Emberton, 'Modern Store Design'.
35. *Den Acht en Opbouw*, 1937, pp. 148–50.
36. Le Corbusier, *Le Modulor*, English translation, London 1954.
37. Carl-Ludwig Franck, conversation with the author, 1974.
38. Theodore Cook, *The Curves of Life*, London 1914.
39. C. H. Reilly, *Architect's Journal*, 18 January 1940.
40. Pleasure Beach Archive. Dated 30 January 1938.
41. *Architectural Review*, July 1939.
42. 'New Style Buildings for Work: Architecture without Extravagance', Derby *Daily Express*, 3 October 1931.
43. *Building*, November 1949.

44. *The Architect's Journal*, 29 November 1956.

45. Serge Chermayeff, letter to the author, 1974.

46. 'London's Buildings Should Tell the Truth', *Evening News*, 18 September 1929.

47. 'It would be greatly for our aesthetic good if we should refrain from the use of ornament for a period of years in order that our thought might concentrate acutely upon the production of buildings well formed and comely in the nude' (*Ornament in Architecture*, 1892).

48. Broadcast in July 1933, printed in *The Listener*, 26 July 1933.

49. W. R. Lethaby, *The Builder*, 6 December 1918.

50. W. R. Lethaby, *The Builder*, 11 October 1918.

51. *Evening News*, 18 September 1929.

PLATES

1 Emberton's, Audley, Staffordshire, in 1974.

2 Joseph Emberton (right) with the sculptor Leon Underwood, a fellow student at the Royal College of Art, dressed for a visit to a pit. (*Jocelyn Emberton Underwood*)

3 Beresford Pite. 82 Mortimer Street, London W1, 1896, in 1975.
4 Beresford Pite. All Souls' School, Foley Street, London W1. Riding House Street elevation, 1906–8, in 1975.

5 Trehearne and Norman. Central House, Kingsway, London EC, *c.* 1913, in 1975.

6 John J. Burnet. Kodak House, Kingsway, London EC, 1911.

7 Thomas Tait. Silver End, Braintree, Essex. Foreman's house, 1928, in 1974.

8 Thomas Tait. Silver End. Le Chateau, 1928, in 1974.

9 Alexander Thomson. Caledonia Road United Presbyterian Church, Glasgow, 1856.

10 W. M. Dudok. Hilversum Town Hall, 1928–32.

11 Louis Sullivan. Guaranty Building, Buffalo, New York, 1895.

12 Burnet and Tait. Adelaide House, London Bridge, 1925, in 1975.

13 Westwood and Emberton. Lakeside kiosks, British Empire Exhibition, Wembley, 1924–25. (*Country Life*)

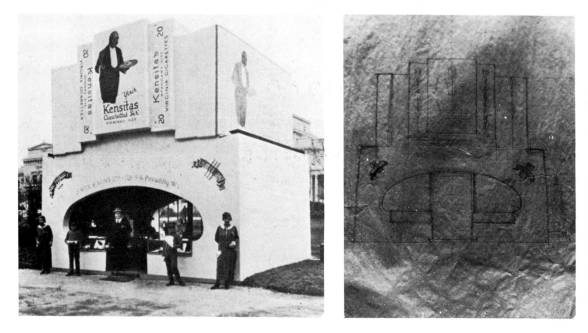

14, 15 Westwood and Emberton. Kensitas lakeside kiosk, British Empire Exhibition, 1924–25. (*Country Life*). Elevation. (*Allan Ure*)

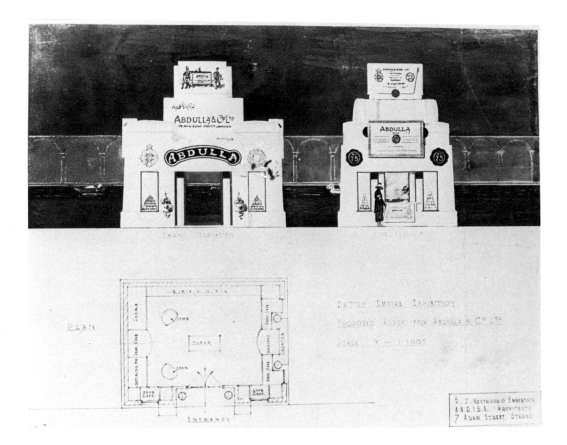

16 Westwood and Emberton. Abdullah lakeside kiosk, British Empire Exhibition, 1924–25.
Elevations and plan. (*Allan Ure*)

17, 18 Westwood and Emberton. London Midland and Scottish Railway enquiry kiosk and Oxo lakeside kiosk, British Empire Exhibition, 1924–25. (*Country Life*)

19 Westwood and Emberton. Back of Eno's kiosk, British Empire Exhibition, 1924–25. (*Country Life*)

20 Westwood and Emberton. State Express pavilion, British Empire Exhibition, 1924–25. (*Country Life*)

21 Westwood and Emberton. State Express pavilion under construction, British Empire exhibition, 1924–25. (*Mrs Emberton*)

22 Westwood and Emberton. House for Mrs Anderson, Churchfields, Weybridge, 1926.
(*Mrs Emberton*)

23 Westwood and Emberton. House for Mrs Anderson, 1926, in 1980.

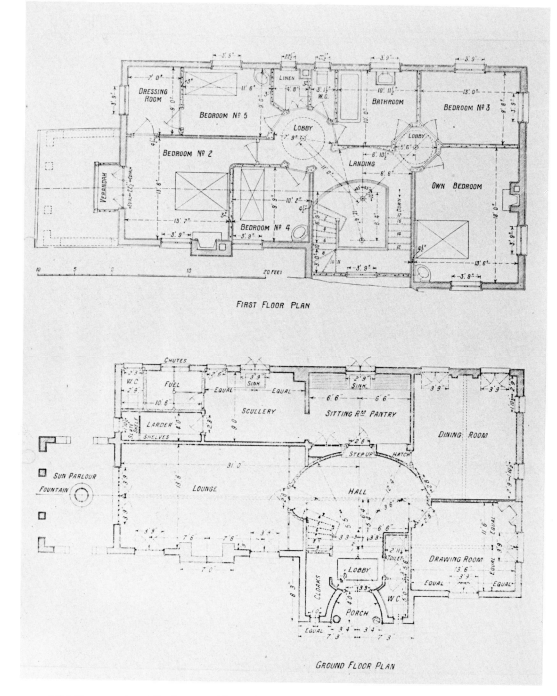

24 Westwood and Emberton. House for Mrs Anderson, 1926. Plans. (*Mrs Emberton*)

25 Westwood and Emberton. House for Mrs Anderson, 1926, roof detail in 1980.

26 J.-M. Olbrich. Villa Friedmann, Hinterbruhl, near Vienna, 1898.

27 Westwood and Emberton. Summit House (for Austin Reed), Red Lion Square, London EC, 1925, in 1976. (*Ray Harrap*)

28 H. H. P. Berlage. Holland House, Bury Street, London EC, 1914–16, in 1976. Corner.

29, 30 H. H. P. Berlage. Holland House, 1914–16, in 1976. Detail of windows, and elevation seen in perspective.

31 Westwood and Emberton. Austin Reed's, Regent Street, London W, 1926.
Lift gates by Percy Metcalf.

32 Joseph Emberton. Madelon Chaumet, 35 Berkeley Street, London W, 1926. (*Mrs Emberton*)

33 Joseph Emberton. Advertising Exhibition, Olympia, London W, 1927. (*Architectural Press*)

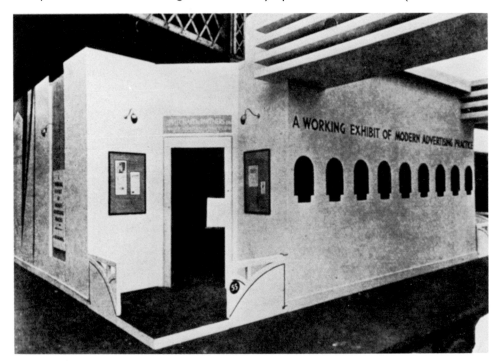

34 Joseph Emberton. Advertising Exhibition, Olympia, 1927. (*Architectural Press*)

35 Joseph Emberton. Advertising Exhibition, Olympia, 1927. (*Architectural Press*)

36 Percy Metcalf. Advertising Association's trophy awarded to Joseph Emberton, 1927.
(*Mrs Emberton*)

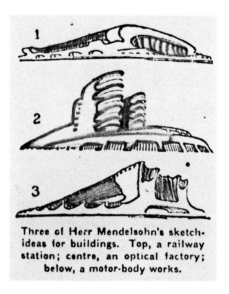

Three of Herr Mendelsohn's sketch-
ideas for buildings. Top, a railway
station; centre, an optical factory;
below, a motor-body works.

37 From 'London's Buildings Should Tell the Truth', *Evening News*, 18 September 1929.

38 Joseph Emberton. Lotus & Delta, Princes Street, Edinburgh, 1928. (*Mrs Emberton*)

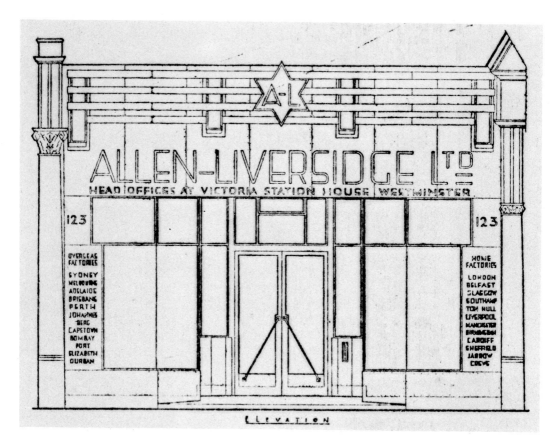

39 Joseph Emberton. Shop for Allen–Liversidge, Victoria Street, London SW1, 1929.
(*Mrs Emberton*)

40 Joseph Emberton. New Empire Hall, Olympia, London W, 1929. Aquatint and dry point by H. T. Brock Grigg. (*Mrs Emberton*)

41 Joseph Emberton. New Empire Hall, Olympia, 1930, in 1974.

42 Joseph Emberton. New Empire Hall, Olympia, 1930, in 1974.

43 Joseph Emberton. New Empire Hall, Olympia, 1930, in 1974. Underside of canopy.

44 Jan Wils. Olympic Stadium, Amsterdam, 1928. (*F. R. Yerbury*)

45 'An Essex Yacht Club: by Joseph Emberton', drawing by William Crabtree shown at the Royal Academy Summer Exhibition in 1930 (no. 1302).

46 Joseph Emberton. Royal Corinthian Yacht Club, 1931. Photograph by Joseph Emberton (?).
(Mrs Emberton)

47 Joseph Emberton. Royal Corinthian Yacht Club, 1931. Photograph by Joseph Emberton (?).
(*Mrs Emberton*)

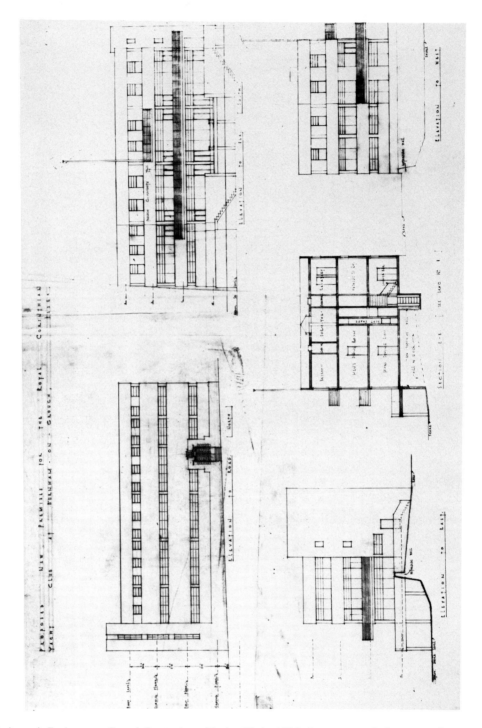

48 Joseph Emberton. Royal Corinthian Yacht Club, 1931. Sections and elevations for an early scheme (2 December 1929). *(RIBA)*

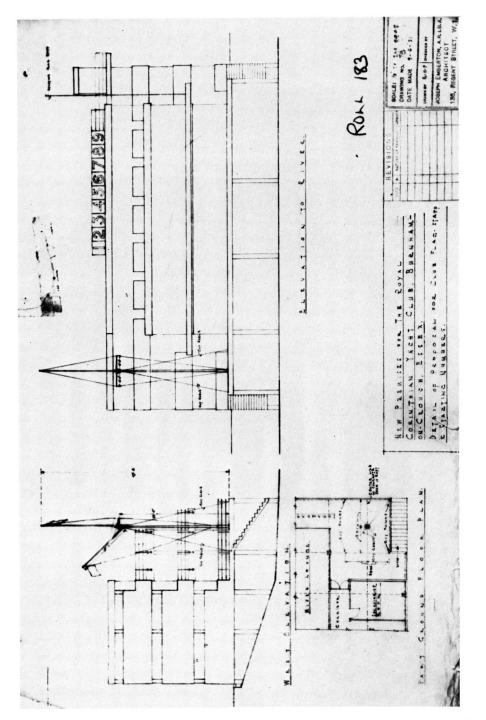

49 Joseph Emberton. Royal Corinthian Yacht Club, 1931. Elevations as built, 9 June 1931.
(RIBA)

50 Joseph Emberton. Royal Corinthian Yacht Club, 1931. Conjunction of side (east) and back (north) elevations. Photograph by Joseph Emberton (?). (*Mrs Emberton*)

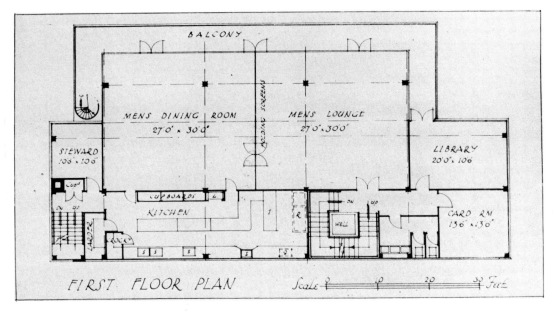

51 Joseph Emberton. Royal Corinthian Yacht Club, 1931. Ground floor plan. (*Mrs Emberton*)

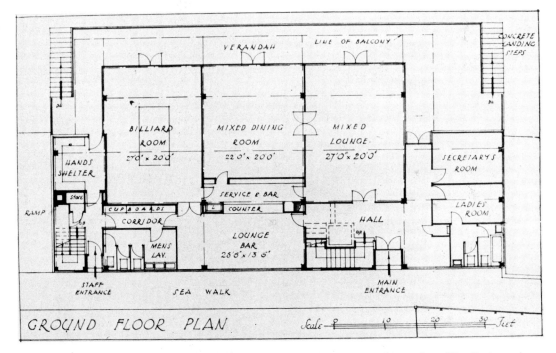

52 Joseph Emberton. Royal Corinthian Yacht Club, 1931. First floor plan. (*Mrs Emberton*)

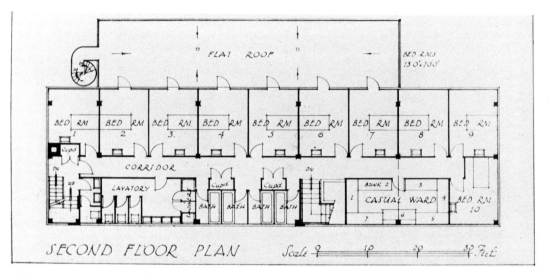

53 Joseph Emberton. Royal Corinthian Yacht Club, 1931. Second floor plan. (*Mrs Emberton*)

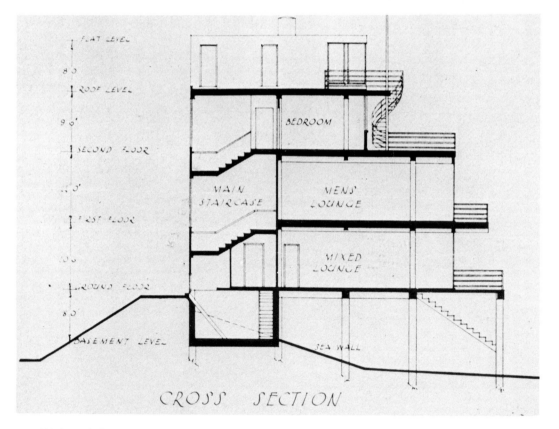

54 Joseph Emberton. Royal Corinthian Yacht Club, 1931. Cross section (*Mrs Emberton*)

55 Joseph Emberton. Royal Corinthian Yacht Club, 1931, in 1974.
Spiral stair with 'Victorian' details.

56 Joseph Emberton. Royal Corinthian Yacht Club, 1931. Diagonal windows of service stair. Photograph by Joseph Emberton(?). (*Mrs Emberton*)

57 Joseph Emberton. Universal House, Southwark Bridge, London SE, 1933, demolished *c.* 1960. (*RIBA*)

58 Joseph Emberton. Universal House, 1933. (*RIBA*)

59 Joseph Emberton. Universal House. From a watercolour by Bob Miller, showing the building extended upwards by six more storeys. (*Robert Miller*)

60 Eric Mendelsohn. Schocken department store, Chemnitz, 1928–29.

61 Joseph Emberton. Ardath Reminder Shop, Regent Street, London W, 1931.

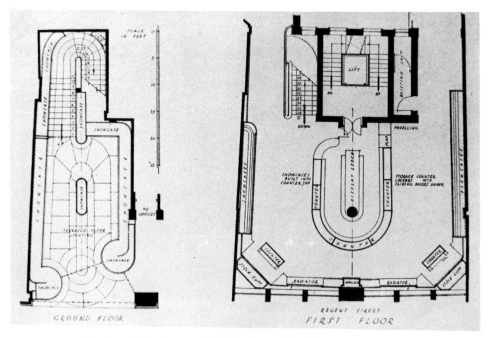

62 Joseph Emberton. Ardath Reminder Shop, 1931. Plans.

63 Joseph Emberton. Advertising Exhibition, Olympia, 1933. (*Architectural Press*)

64 Joseph Emberton. Advertising Exhibition, Olympia, 1933. (*Architectural Press*)

65 Joseph Emberton. Advertising Exhibition, Olympia, 1933. (*Architectural Press*)

66 Joseph Emberton. BTH Refrigerators, Regent Street, London W, 1931.
(*Architectural Association*)

67 Joseph Emberton. BTH Refrigerators, 1931. (*Architectural Association*)

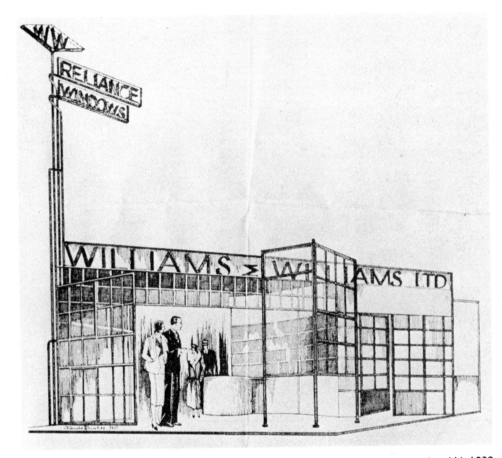

68 Joseph Emberton. Williams & Williams exhibition stand, Olympia, London W, 1932.
(Mrs Emberton)

69 Joseph Emberton. Pleasure Beach, Blackpool. Site in 1935. (*Blackpool Pleasure Beach*)

70 Joseph Emberton. Pleasure Beach, Blackpool, 1935. The Fun House. (*RIBA*)

71 Joseph Emberton. Pleasure Beach, Blackpool, 1935. The Grand National. (*RIBA*)

72 Joseph Emberton. Simpson's, Piccadilly, London W, 1936. Photograph c. 1936.
The name, in coloured neon designed by Eric Gill, is still to be added. (*Mrs Emberton*)

73 Joseph Emberton. Simpson's, Piccadilly, 1936. Welded plate girders with end restraint removed by order of London County Council. Photograph taken in 1935. (*Felix Samuely & Partners, Structural Engineers*)

74 Joseph Emberton. Simpson's, Piccadilly, 1936. Light fitting. (*Simpson (Piccadilly) Ltd*)

75 Joseph Emberton. Simpson's, Piccadilly, 1936. Shirt shop. (*Simpson (Piccadilly) Ltd*)

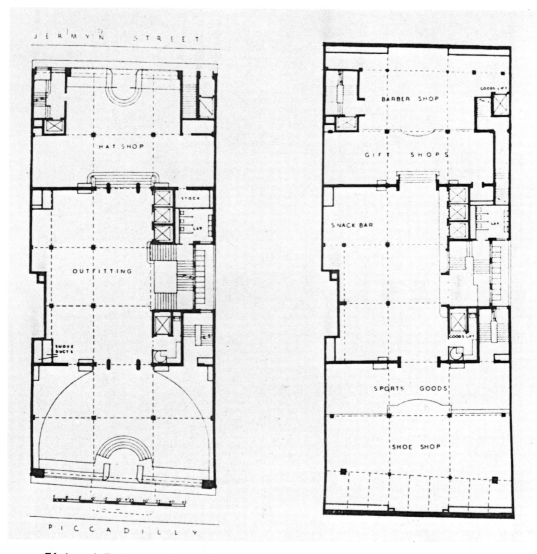

76 Joseph Emberton. Simpson's, Piccadilly, 1936. Ground floor and basement plan. (*Simpson (Piccadilly) Ltd*)

77 Joseph Emberton. Simpson's, Piccadilly, 1936, in 1974. Light fitting in stairwell.

78 Joseph Emberton. Simpson's, Piccadilly, 1936, in 1974. Metal tube and plywood trousers table, by Emberton (?). (*Mrs Emberton*)

79 H. Th. Wijdeveld. Netherlands Pavilion International Exhibition, Antwerp, 1930.
(*F. R. Yerbury*)

80 J. Duiker. Gooiland Hotel, Hilversum, 1934–36. Sketch, January 1935.

81 Joseph Emberton. Timothy White's, Southsea, 1934. (*Architectural Press*)

82 Joseph Emberton. Chapman House, Chapman Street, Stepney, London E, 1934. (*RIBA*)

83 Joseph Emberton. Turnour House, Stepney, London E, 1934, in 1974.

84 Joseph Emberton. Turnour House, 1934, in 1974.

85 Joseph Emberton. Soleil Pavilion, Paris International Exhibition, 1937. (*Mrs Emberton*)

86 Joseph Emberton. Soleil Pavilion at night, 1937. (*Mrs Emberton*)

87 Thomas Tait. Glasgow International Exhibition, 1938. 'Tait's Tower' and Garden Club. Emberton's British Railways pavilion is on the left. (*Mitchell Library, Glasgow*)

88 Eric Mendelsohn and Serge Chermayeff. De la Warr Pavilion, Bexhill, Sussex, 1936. (*Jane Beckett*)

89 Joseph Emberton. His Master's Voice shop, Oxford Street, London W, 1939, in 1974.

90 Joseph Emberton. HMV shop, 1939. Stair. (*Architectural Press*)

91 Joseph Emberton. Eardley House, Alsager Road, Audley, Staffordshire, 1939, in 1974.

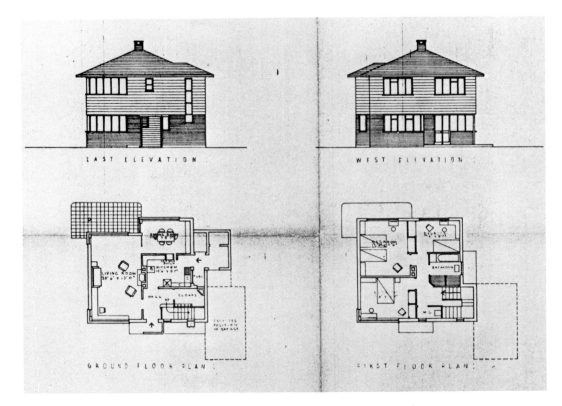

92 Joseph Emberton. Eardley House, 1939. Elevations and plans.

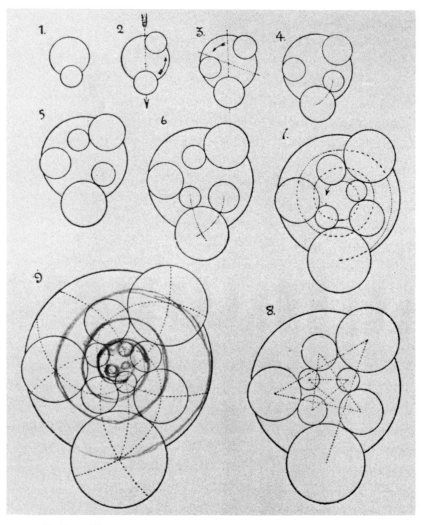

93 From Theodore Cook, *The Curves of Life* (London 1914).

94 Joseph Emberton. New Casino and Pleasure Beach, Blackpool, 1939. Early design drawing. *(Blackpool Pleasure Beach)*

95 Joseph Emberton. Blackpool Casino, 1939. The top storey has not yet been added. *(RIBA)*

96 Joseph Emberton. Blackpool Casino, 1939, in 1974. 'Sun parlour' on roof.

97 Joseph Emberton. Blackpool Casino in course of construction. (*Blackpool Pleasure Beach*)

98 Joseph Emberton. Blackpool Casino, 1939. (*Blackpool Pleasure Beach*)

99 Joseph Emberton. Blackpool Casino, 1939. Main stair. (*Blackpool Pleasure Beach*)

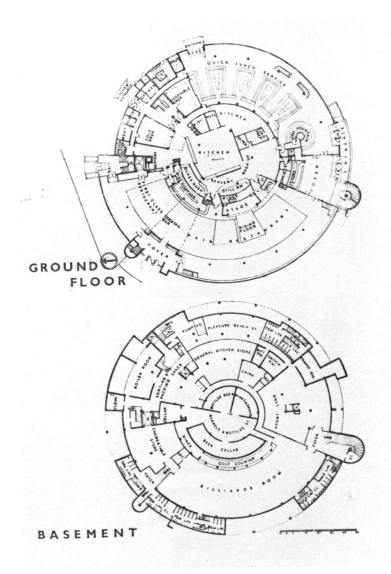

GROUND
FLOOR

BASEMENT

100 Joseph Emberton. Blackpool Casino, 1939. Plan basement and ground floor.
(*Architectural Press*)

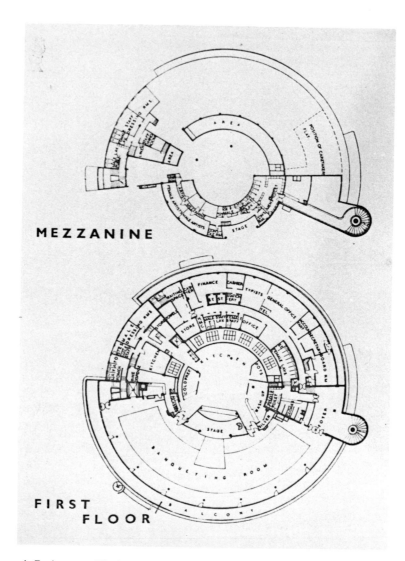

MEZZANINE

**FIRST
FLOOR**

101 Joseph Emberton. Blackpool Casino, 1939. Plan first floor and mezzanine floor.
(*Architectural Press*)

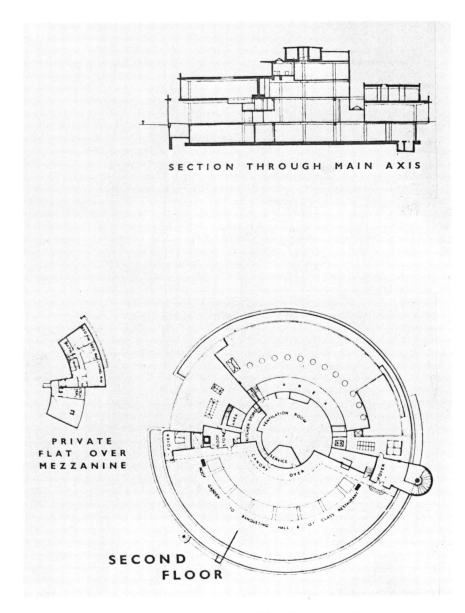

SECTION THROUGH MAIN AXIS

PRIVATE
FLAT OVER
MEZZANINE

SECOND
FLOOR

102 Joseph Emberton. Blackpool Casino, 1939. Plan second floor and section.
(*Architectural Press*)

103 Joseph Emberton. Blackpool Casino, 1939. Bedside cabinet. (*Blackpool Pleasure Beach*)

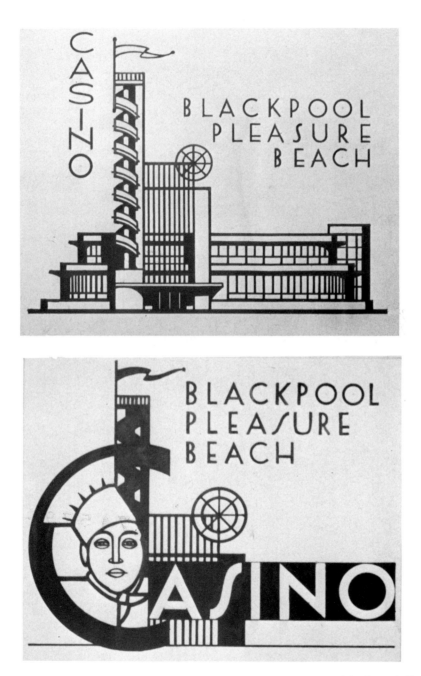

104, 105 Blackpool Casino. Advertising and decorations commissioned by Joseph Emberton.

106, 107 Advertising and decorations commissioned by Joseph Emberton.

108, 109 Advertising and decorations commissioned by Joseph Emberton.

110, 111 Advertising and decorations commissioned by Joseph Emberton.

112, 113 Advertising and decorations commissioned by Joseph Emberton.

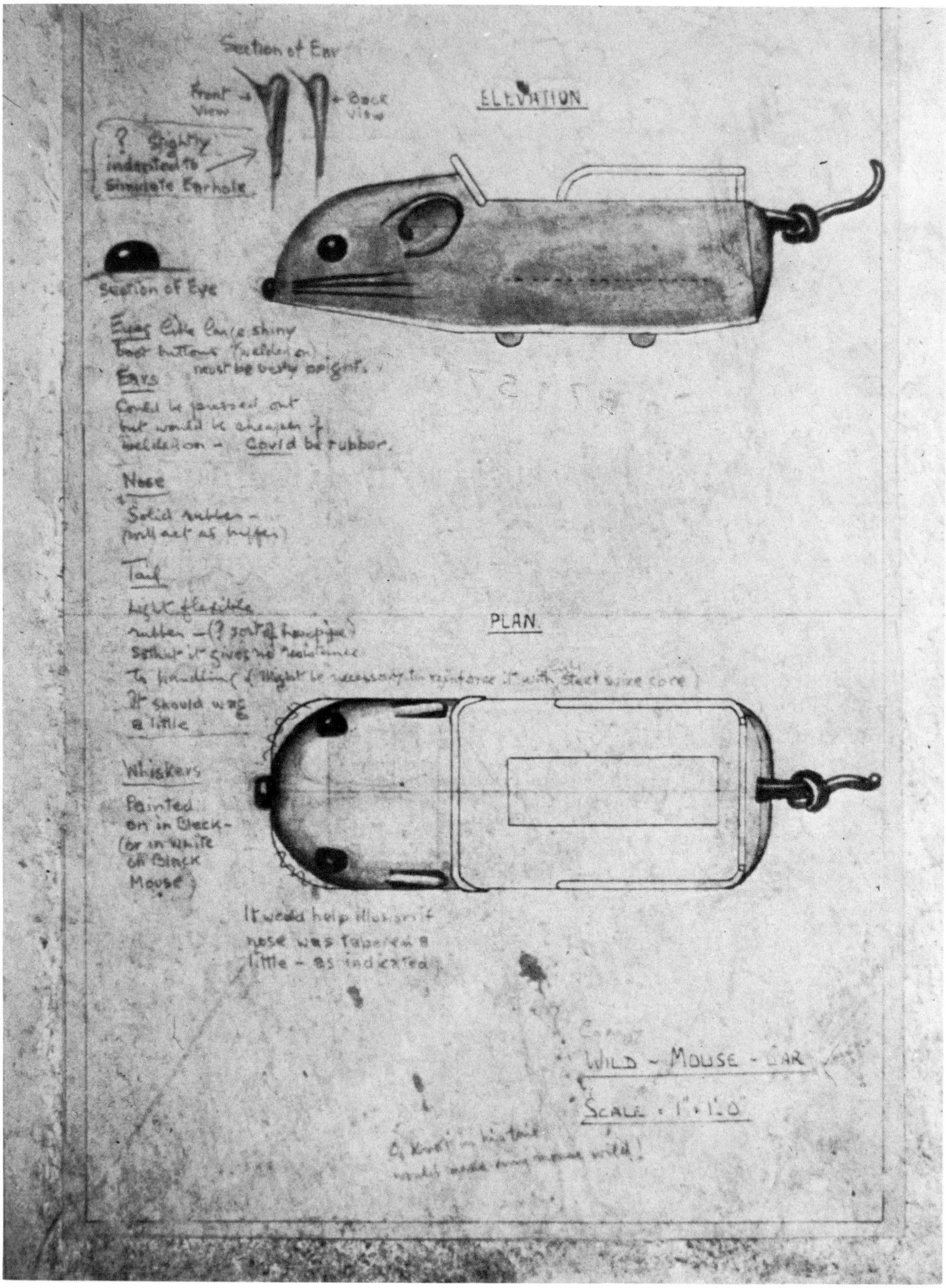

Section of Ear

Front → ← Back
View View

? Slightly
indented to
simulate Earhole.

ELEVATION

Section of Eye

Eyes little large shiny
boot buttons (welded on)
must be very bright.

Ears
Could be pressed out
but would be cheaper of
fabrication — could be rubber.

Nose
Solid rubber —
(will act as buffer)

Tail
light & flexible
rubber — (? sort of hosepipe)
so that it gives no resistance
in handling (might be necessary to reinforce it with steel wire core)
It should wag
a little

Whiskers
Painted
on in Black —
(or in white
off Black
Mouse)

PLAN.

It would help illusion if
nose was tapered a
little — as indicated.

WILD - MOUSE - CAR

SCALE : 1" = 1'0"

A kink in his tail
would make him more wild!

114 Blackpool Casino. Plan and elevation of Wild Mouse.

115 Schneider Trophy winner, Supermarine S6B. Outright winner of the trophy for the Royal Aero Club, 1931. (*Science Museum*)

116 Joseph Emberton. Steel house prototype, 1946. (*Mrs Emberton*)

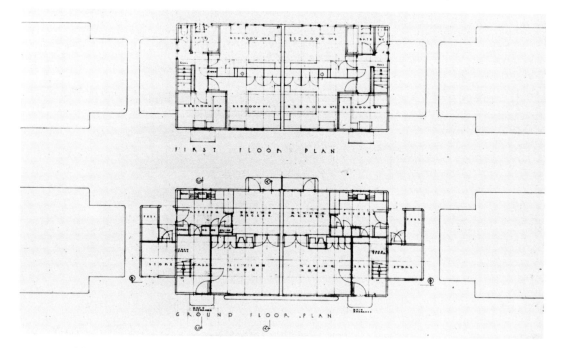

117 Joseph Emberton. Steel house prototype, 1946. Plans. (*Mrs Emberton*)

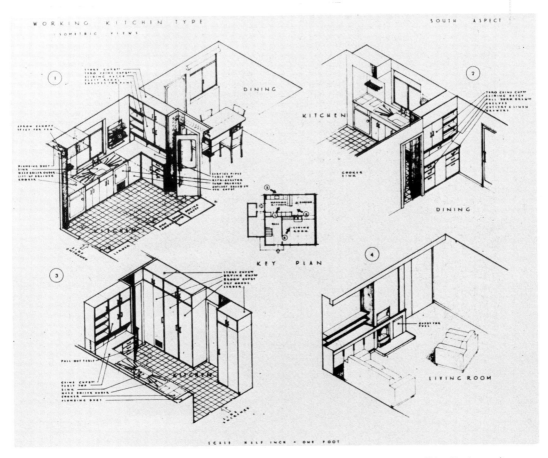

118 Joseph Emberton. Steel house prototype, 1946. Axonometrics. (*Mrs Emberton*)

119 Joseph Emberton. Easiwork factory, near Maidstone, Kent, 1949. (*Mrs Emberton*)

120 Joseph Emberton. Stuart Mill House, Killick Street, London N, 1954, in 1974.

121 Joseph Emberton. Stafford Cripps Estate, Old Street, London EC, 1954, in 1974.

122 Joseph Emberton. Stafford Cripps Estate, 1954, in 1974.

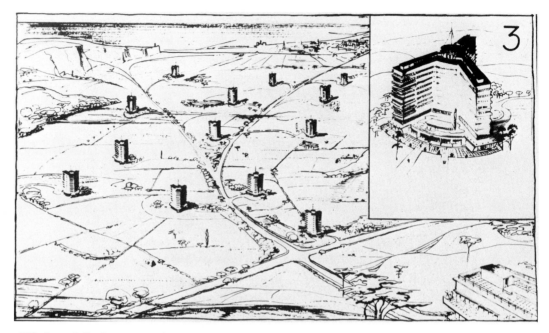

123 Joseph Emberton. Proposal for rebuilding the Paternoster site. Drawing by Carl-Ludwig Franck. (*Mrs Emberton*)

124 Joseph Emberton. Proposal for rebuilding the Paternoster site. Drawing by Carl-Ludwig Franck. (*Mrs Emberton*)

125 Joseph Emberton, *c.* 1954. (*Mrs Emberton*)